Physical Change and Aging

A Guide for the Helping Professions

Sue V. Saxon
Ph.D., Professor, Aging Studies Program, University of South Florida, Tampa, Florida

Mary Jean Etten
R.N., Ed.D., Associate Professor of Nursing and Gerontology, St. Petersburg Junior College, St. Petersburg, Florida

THE TIRESIAS PRESS, NEW YORK

To our parents
ESTON L. and MILDRED Z. SAXON
HENRY and AMANDA ETTEN

Library of Congress
Catalog Card Number: 77-93112
International Standard
Book Number: 0-913292-12-5

Printed in U.S.A.

Current printing (last digit): 10 9 8 7 6 5 4 2 1

Contents

Preface

As instructors of gerontology, we have given many courses, workshops, and speeches on the aging process. In our experience, the one basic area of aging that is either presented in highly technical terms beyond general comprehension or else skimmed over superficially is that which examines the physical changes associated with aging.

This book is intended primarily for those in the helping professions—nurses, social workers, psychologists, clergy, counselors, and others—who would like a better understanding of the physical aspects of aging and their implications for behavior. It can be used as a text for those who have a limited science background or as a training manual for workshops and inservice education. Others, who would simply like to know more about aging, or how to cope effectively with their own individual aging, may also find it useful.

Although this book focuses on the physical changes that occur with age, it also considers the psychological and social implications of such changes for human behavior. Since aging is a complex process, it is impossible to consider its biological aspects without a comparable concern for the emotional and social problems that attend it.

To achieve our aim of conciseness, we have organized the material into three parts. Part I deals with general thoughts on the aging process. In Part II we discuss each organ system of the body from the standpoints of normal system functions, specific age-related changes in the system, and, briefly, the major age-related diseases or disorders of the system. Since there is some disagreement as to what constitutes "normal" aging as opposed to pathology or disease among the aged, age-related changes cited in this book are those that appear in more than one authoritative reference source. Part III deals with a number of other topics, including nutrition, exercise, and homeostasis, that relate to physical change and age. The appendixes give suggestions on safety, self-help, and sources of more specific information. At the end of each unit we have included a selective bibliography to guide the interested reader into more detailed and specific material.

This book is not intended to serve as a scholarly text, but rather as a concise summary of the significant aspects of physical change and age and, we hope, as a stimulus for additional reading in greater depth.

We would like to express our appreciation to R. Douglas Bailey for the illustrations, to Grace Patterson, who cheerfully typed and retyped the manuscript, to Gary Lyman for reading sections of the manuscript, to Thomas A. Rich, who provided administrative support and encouragement to the project during the past year, and to Mildred Z. Saxon, who read all of the numerous drafts and who maintained a calm, tranquil, and supportive atmosphere for us during the entire period of our efforts.

SUE V. SAXON
MARY JEAN ETTEN
February, 1978

Part I

Unit 1

Introduction

The study of the aging process is a relatively new area of concern and investigation, but one that is growing rapidly. Hendricks and Hendricks (1) report that in 1940 there were some five or six basic books and about a hundred journal articles on aging, whereas a recent attempt to compile a bibliography of the literature published between 1954 and 1974 unearthed approximately 50,000 references.

The two academic specialties evolving from this intensified interest are *gerontology,* the study of the aging process, and *geriatrics,* the study of medical problems associated with growing older. Geriatrics is a branch of medicine, while gerontology utilizes multidisciplinary and interdisciplinary approaches in an attempt to understand all facets of aging.

Atchley (2) contends that aging is a newly defined social problem in our society, resulting from population changes, urbanization, industrialization, and fast-paced social change. Population changes have undoubtedly had a substantial impact in making the elderly more visible and their needs more obvious. In 1900 there were about three million people over age 65 in the United States; in 1970 there were more than 20 million Americans over 65. Due to declining mortality at all ages and to immigration, the older population has been increasing more rapidly during this century than other age groups. Projections suggest that by 1990 the aged population will have increased about 38 percent over that of 1970, and that by 2000 there will be an estimated 29 million Americans who are 65 and over. In addition, many more people are reaching very old age. In 1900, approximately 29 percent of the aged population was over 75; in 1970, 39 percent was over 75, and estimates indicate that by 2000 almost 44 percent of the older population will be over 75 (3).

Since more people are reaching older age than ever before, gerontologists and providers of services to older persons are finding it necessary to redefine the concept of "old age." Bernice Neugarten (4) has suggested that it is more appropriate to think of those who are 55 to 74 as the "young-old" and those who are 75 and over as the "old-old." Certainly most service providers agree that, since needs are generally different in the young-old and old-old groups, services and programs should be planned, oriented, and delivered in different ways. Ollie Randall (5) emphasizes the broad chronological age range of the elderly today by suggesting the following categories: "very-young-old" (50 to 60), "young-old" (61 to 70), "middle-aged-old" (71 to 80), "very-old-old" (81 to 99), and "centenarians" for the increasing number of those who are 100 and over. Although both Neugarten and Randall agree that chronological age is not an accurate predictor of physical condition and behavior, their suggestions focus attention upon the great diversity in the group we call "old" and point out that differentiations must be made in this large, heterogeneous segment of the population if we are to provide effectively for human needs throughout the life span. People become more unique as they grow older, not more alike. Because of this, and because aging is a distinct part of the life cycle not yet personally experienced by most of those who work with the elderly, understanding the behavior of aged persons is difficult for many in the helping professions. In our attempts to understand others, we often lean heavily on our personal experiences and can, therefore, empathize reasonably well with a child, adolescent, young adult, or middle-ager. To understand the perspective of older individuals, however, it is necessary to project ourselves into an age context with which we have no personal experience. Ollie Randall sums up the need as follows: "The greatest priority for older people is the ability and opportunity to create a quality of living that is consonant with an individual's wishes. This takes more than money—and often does not require money at all. It takes understanding of that which gives satisfaction in being alive"(6).

Aging should be viewed in a developmental perspective, as a natural part of the life cycle, with the many experiences of earlier years as well as present life situations all contributing to behavior in the later years. There is no such phenomenon as an "old age personality"; rather, as people grow older they tend to become more of what they have always been. Actually, there have been few efforts to systematically study the entire life cycle, and most developmental theories have stopped at adolescence. As Bromley says: "We spend about one quarter of our lives growing up and three quarters growing old" (7). It seems strange, then, that psychologists and others interested in human development have devoted the majority of their efforts to the study of childhood and adolescence.

In spite of the lack of research data, some attempts have been made to systematize developmental tasks that encompass the entire life span. These attempts are based on the assumption that rather specific tasks are expected to be encountered and mastered at certain points or stages in the life cycle. Failure to resolve developmental tasks at the appropriate time presumably interferes with personal-social adaptation and with adjustment to the next stage and its tasks. Although this approach is not acceptable to all and research is sparse, the developmental task view does provide guidelines to society's expectations for individual behavior at different ages and may therefore be useful in suggesting clues to follow in assessing behavior and adaptation throughout the life cycle.

Erik Erikson (8) proposed one classification of developmental tasks ranging from the development of a sense of basic trust (versus a sense of mistrust) in infancy to the development of a sense of ego integrity (versus a sense of despair) in old age. The developmental perspective presented below has been suggested by Brammer and Shostrom (9), to which we have added information from Bernice Neugarten (10) concerning middle age periods.

0-2 INFANCY: *Dependency* stage, when the infant learns to relate to caretakers on whom it is at first totally dependent. Earliest experiences with human relationships occur here.

2-3 EARLY CHILDHOOD: *Independence* stage, when the child acquires an increasing sense of autonomy, independence, and mastery. Walking and talking aid significantly in mobility, in intensified exploration of the environment, and in building more complex relationships with others. Toilet training is extremely important in our culture because it is possibly the first time the child has to acquiesce to the demands of authority figures. Management of aggression is another culturally expected behavior at this time.

4-6 MIDDLE CHILDHOOD: *Role taking,* in which the relevant task is to learn proper social roles, especially sex roles. Conscience development is also a significant aspect of development at this age level.

6-10 LATE CHILDHOOD: *Conformity,* when the child must learn to cope with new authority figures and heterogeneous peers as a result of school experiences. Preference for same sex friends and associations is characteristic of this age.

10-13 PREADOLESCENCE: *Transition* stage, dominated by adjustment to rapid physical growth, sexual maturation, and increased efforts to become independent of family control. Sense of individuality is usually strong at this time, but peer pressure and peer conformity begin to increase.

13-20 ADOLESCENCE: *Synthesis* stage, extremely significant

in our culture since the transition from child to adult generally occurs during this stage. Unfortunately, our culture has no clearly defined and universally acceptable guidelines for determining when the transition is completed; thus adults, especially parents, may not behave consistently toward the adolescent who in one situation is considered to be an adult but in another similar situation may be treated as a child. Neither parents, friends, society, nor the adolescent knows when the transition to adult status has been completed and this uncertainty increases the possibility of conflict. In addition, many important life decisions are made at this time such as career choice, education, marriage, parenthood, establishment of an independent life style, and personal identity. Establishing a firm sense of personal identity and independence become paramount.

20-35 EARLY ADULT: *Experimentation,* in which young people test their decisions against reality. For many, this is the first opportunity for decisions made in the earlier stage to be tried out in real life situations. The individual begins to be established as an independent young adult testing self against realities of work, of home, of civic, religious, and recreational involvements, and of interpersonal relationships.

35-50 MIDDLE AGE: *Consolidation stage.* For many middle-agers this is a time for intensive reevaluation of self and life. Middle age involves a changing time perspective with the realization that half of one's life is over.

45-60 MIDDLE AGE: *Involutional stage,* which overlaps in age range with the consolidation stage. The developmental emphasis here is specifically on coping with the psychological implications of impending old age. Menopause in women and climacteric changes in men, gray hair, wrinkles, lessened energy and stamina are all physical signs of age. Some middle-agers experience depression as a number of psychologically significant events cumulate at about this point in the life cycle: children leave home, career and financial abilities peak, awareness of physical signs of age occurs, parents and friends begin to die, and time perspective changes as half the life has been lived. For those who fear old age and death, depression and psychological problems are likely to occur. For those who perceive their lives as rewarding and fulfilling, middle age is a highly satisfying period. Many cope by finding new interests, intensifying current interests, and setting new priorities for use of time; others make drastic changes in their life style (divorce after 20 to 30 years of marriage is on the increase); others have a "last fling" of infidelity to prove their sexual prowess and attractiveness; and some experience emotional breakdown. One group of educated and articulate middle-agers studied by Neugarten (11) stressed that middle age is a time of competence and mastery, the prime of life—a comfortable period of life indeed.

60 AND OLDER: *Evaluation stage.* The major tasks of the older age stage are to work through a life review—a purposive, constructive effort to review one's life to put it into perspective—and to cope with cumulating losses that usually occur with advancing age. A sense of personal integrity, the comfort of a life well lived, and preparation for easy death are important achievements during this period.

Human behavior involves complex interrelationships between physical, psychological, and social factors. Both the nature and significance of bio-psycho-social interrelationships change as aging occurs. Each individual remains a unique and complex being throughout life and can only be properly understood from a holistic perspective.

Unit 2

Theories
of
Aging

No one knows exactly how or why aging occurs, although numerous theories of biological aging have been proposed. No one theory is currently acceptable as an adequate explanation of the aging process. Much of the available research in this area involves subhuman species and thus generalizability to humans is open to question.

Several of the present theories are not now amenable to satisfactory experimental verification due to limitations in available methodology.

In brief, the best known hypotheses or theories of biological aging involve the following:

GENETIC FACTORS THEORY

Life span is presumed to be determined by a fixed program in the genes of body cells; specifically, by a code in the DNA (deoxyribonucleic acid) contained in the genes. Life span appears to be fixed from species to species; in humans it is estimated to be approximately 110 to 115 years. The best known support for genetic viewpoints is the work of Hayflick, who investigated certain body cells maintained in tissue cultures outside the body (12). He observed that cells taken from old animals divide only about 20 to 25 times, then die, whereas cells from young animals normally divide 40 or 50 times. Hayflick's data are often quoted as evidence that a species' life span is fixed and genetically determined at the level of the cell. There is not clear evidence, though, that this particular type of cell activity occurs in the same way in the intact living organism.

SOMATIC MUTATION THEORIES

One mutation theory is concerned with the effect of sublethal radiation on aging. Several types of evidence suggest that radiation exposure accelerates the aging process. If we assume that radiation causes abnormal changes in genes, or mutations, then it is possible that mutated cells are unable to perform their normal functions and the body is affected adversely.

ERROR THEORY

Information in the genetic code must be transmitted properly for the system to operate efficiently. DNA stores such information and RNA (ribonucleic acid) is necessary for its transmission. If errors occur in the "copying" process, inaccurate genetic information is copied and transmitted, impairing cell function. According to error theory, aging and death are the result of errors occurring and transmitted at the cellular level. Error theory is currently stimulating a substantial amount of basic research.

WEAR AND TEAR THEORY

Wear and tear theory is an older viewpoint based on the assumption that continued use leads to worn out or defective parts. This position ignores the various repair mechanisms available in the body and the fact that, in some cases, use contributes to increased strength (in muscles, for example).

ACCUMULATION THEORIES

These theories emphasize possible accumulation of certain substances in body cells as a result of age. Theoretically, over-accumulation of these substances decreases cell efficiency until the cell becomes inoperative and dies. The most commonly noted substance that collects in body cells with age is lipofuscin.

Additional research is needed to demonstrate the actual effects of substance buildup as there is little clear evidence so far of impaired cell functioning due strictly to accumulating materials in cells with age.

CROSS-LINKING THEORY

Elastin and collagen (connective tissues that support and connect body organs and structures) figure prominently in this theoretical perspective. Both form cross-linking or bonds with age, resulting in rigidity and less pliability of the connective tissue. Effective functioning of body organs and structures depends upon some degree of elasticity of the supporting tissues. Collagen accounts for approximately one-third of all the protein in the body and thus assumes functional significance for mobility in general. The pertinent questions of most importance for this theoretical position are whether cross-linking occurs throughout the entire body as a function of age and what impact cross-linking has on effective functioning of specific body systems.

STRESS THEORY

Elaborated mostly by Selye (13), stress theory suggests that each bit of stress leaves in the organism some residual impairment which accumulates over the lifetime until body reserves are depleted. This theoretical position has engendered much discussion, research, and controversy, but has not been generally accepted as an entirely adequate explanation of the aging process at this time.

IMMUNE SYSTEM THEORY

The immune system of the body protects against invading organisms. It also protects against mutant cells within the body by producing antibodies that attack and destroy the abnormal cells. According to this theory of aging, the body's immune system may change in one or more ways with age: a) antibodies may be produced that destroy normal body cells; b) antibodies may not recognize mutated cells and may allow deviant cells to grow and develop; and c) older organisms may not be able to produce enough antibodies to destroy intruders. This theoretical approach is regarded as promising by current researchers.

BIBLIOGRAPHY

Books

Bondareff, William. The neural basis of aging. In Birren, James E. and Schaie, K. Warner, eds., *Handbook of the Psychology of Aging.* New York: Van Nostrand Reinhold, 1977.

Busse, Ewald. *Theories of aging.* In Busse, Ewald and Pfeiffer, Eric, eds., *Behavior and Adaptation in Late Life.* Boston: Little, Brown, 1969.

Finch, Caleb E. Biological theories of aging. In Burnside, Irene M., ed., *Nursing and the Aged.* New York: McGraw-Hill, 1976.

Hershey, Daniel. *Lifespan and Factors Affecting It.* Springfield, Ill.: Charles C Thomas, 1974.

Kohn, Robert R. *Principles of Mammalian Aging.* Englewood Cliffs, N.J.: Prentice-Hall, 1971.

Makinodan, Takashi. Immunity and aging. In Finch, Caleb E. and Hayflick, Leonard, eds., *Handbook of the Biology of Aging.* New York: Van Nostrand Reinhold, 1977.

Shock, Nathan W. Biological theories of aging. In Birren, James E. and Schaie, K. Warner, eds., *Handbook of the Psychology of Aging.* op. cit.

Spiegel, Paul M. Theories of aging. In Timiras, P. S., ed., *Developmental Physiology and Aging.* New York: Macmillan, 1972.

Periodicals

Adler, W. H. Aging and immune function. *Bioscience 25:*652, 1975.

Bjorksten, J. The crosslinkage theory of aging. *Journal of the American Geriatrics Society 16:*408, 1968.

Burch, P. R. Immunological aspects of aging. *Practitioner 214:*533, 1975.

Comfort, Alex. Biological theories of aging. *Human Development 13:*127, 1970.

Gelfant, S. and Smith, J. G. Aging: noncycling cells an explanation. *Science 178:*357, 1972.

Goldstein, S. Biological aging. An essentially normal process. *Journal of the American Medical Association 230:*1651, 1974.

Hayflick, Leonard. Aging under glass.*Experimental Gerontology 5:*291, 1970.

Hayflick, Leonard. Cell biology of aging. *Bioscience 25:*629, 1975.

Hayter, J. Biologic changes of aging. *Nursing Forum 13:*289, 1974.

Makinodan, T. Immunobiology of aging. *Journal of the American Geriatrics Society 24:*249, 1976.

Manley, G. The biology of aging. *Nursing Times 71:*246, 1975.

Robert, L. and Robert, B. Immunology and aging. *Gerontologica Clinica 19:*330, 1973.

Walford, Roy, The immunologic theory of aging. *Gerontologist 4:*195, 1964.

Wallace, D. J. The biology of aging: 1976, an overview. *Journal of the American Geriatrics Society 25:*104, 1977.

Part II

Unit 3

The
Skin
(Integument)

Although not often identified as a body system, the skin and its appendages (hair, nails, sweat and oil glands) is one of the largest and most complicated of the body systems. The skin surface of an average adult covers over 3,000 square inches, weighs about six pounds, is served by one-third of all the blood circulating in the body, and contains many nerves and sensory receptors (14).

COMPONENTS

The three layers of tissue comprising the skin are the epidermis, the dermis, and the subcutaneous layer.

● *The epidermis,* or outer layer, contains many dead cells which are constantly being scraped off and replaced by new cells from below. Protection against bacterial invasion and ultraviolet rays (from the sun) is the prime function of the epidermis. A pigment (melanin) located in the epidermis determines skin color.

● The intermediate layer, or *dermis,* contains nerves, blood vessels, hair follicles, sweat and oil glands.

● The innermost layer, or *subcutaneous layer,* contains blood vessels, nerves, and fat. Fat in subcutaneous tissues decreases with age, causing a wrinkling of skin surfaces.

FUNCTIONS

Basic functions of skin are:

1.   Protection of underlying tissues and structures.
2.   Sensory reception, especially for touch, pain, and pressure.
3.   Temperature regulation through the mechanisms of sweating and shivering.
4.   Prevention of tissue drying or excessive loss of water throughout the body.

Age-Related Changes in the Skin

The most obvious age-related change in the skin is wrinkling, caused by loss of skin elasticity and decreased subcutaneous fat. Aging skin develops folds and becomes flabby in appearance.

Two other noticeable changes normally occurring with age are graying and loss of hair. Both graying and baldness are to some extent genetically determined. Baldness is more common in males, but hair also becomes thinner in some females. Although neither wrinkling nor loss of hair have important implications for physical health, these are among the first and most obvious signs of impending old age. Facial hair sometimes

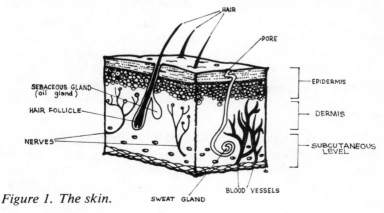

Figure 1. The skin.

increases, an age-related change especially bothersome to females over 40 who adhere to our present cultural standards of beauty. Such markers may have enormous psychological significance for some individuals and it is therefore necessary to understand the highly personal meaning of visible age-related changes.

Brown pigmented spots appear on the backs of hands, wrists, and to some extent, on the face. These are frequently referred to as "age spots" or "liver spots." They are unrelated to the liver, though, and are benign, harmless, pigmented areas properly identified as *lentigo senilus.*

Small hemorrhages occur under the skin due to the thinness of skin and increasing fragility of small blood vessels, resulting in red blotches on skin surfaces. These are usually not considered to be health problems unless caused by trauma sufficient to break the skin. In such cases healing may be slower than in younger persons and infection more likely.

A change of greater significance but one frequently overlooked in health information for the elderly relates to nail care, which has definite implications for locomotion and total mobility. Fingernails and toenails become tough and brittle with age and may not be cut properly or as often as necessary. In fact, one item in a well known checklist that is used to assess the ability of older people to live independently is whether or not they can cut their own toenails, a task requiring body flexibility, coordination, and adequate vision (15). Both foot discomfort and unnecessary infections can be caused by improper nail care.

Age-Related Disorders of the Skin

Pruritus (Itching)

Pruritus is a frequently observed and often intense skin ailment in older persons. A common site is the legs, but it may be present on any part of the body. As skin becomes thinner and dryer it is more susceptible to such irritants as soap, tight clothing, woolens, changes in weather, cosmetics, drugs, and prickly heat. Itching can also be a symptom of more serious health situations such as liver disease, cancer, leukemia, diabetes, uremia, thyroid, or mental disorders, and should not be ignored.

Cancer of the Skin

The incidence of skin cancer increases with age and is especially prevalent in the seventh, eighth, and ninth decades. Prolonged exposure to sunlight and chronic irritants such as eyeglasses, pipes, or clothing serve as precipitating factors. *Basal cell* and *squamous cell* cancers are most commonly found in the elderly. Basal cell cancer may be identified as a small, flat, smooth, or solid elevated lesion with scales or crusts that bleeds easily. Usually located on the face, this cancer invades nearby tissue but rarely spreads to other parts of the body. In contrast, squamous cell cancers are solid, elevated lesions on the face that grow rapidly and quickly spread to the lymph nodes. A third type of skin cancer, *malignant melanoma,* is a highly malignant cancer that develops slowly. It may be flat or elevated with irregular margins and is colored blue, black, tan, brown, white, or pink. Any change in size or coloration of a mole or symptoms such as itching or bleeding indicate the need for immediate medical attention. This cancer is only curable when it has not spread beyond the primary lesion.

Although thousands of new cases of skin cancer develop each year, the rate of cure is about 95 percent. Any changes in skin or moles, however, should be inspected by a physician as cure depends on early diagnosis and effective treatment.

Keratoses (Horny Overgrowths)

Two types of keratoses are found in the elderly: *seborrheic* keratosis and *senile* keratosis. Seborrheic keratosis resembles a yellowish or brownish wart covered by a greasy scale. Persons who have oily skins are more prone to develop this condition although it seldom becomes malignant. Senile keratosis is characterized by raised brown or gray areas that become scaly. These lesions should be removed as they can become malignant.

Stasis Ulcer

Stasis ulcer is caused by varicose veins and poor venous return. The lower leg is a common site. The disease is characterized by edema and swelling plus a bluish-red discloration causing itching, scratching, possible infection, and possible ulcers. Obesity, sedentary occupations, and tight garters contribute to ulcer formation. Long-term treatment may be needed.

Decubitus Ulcers (Bedsores)

Skin breakdown results from prolonged pressure on bony areas of the body. Since many elderly people have thin skin, less subcutaneous fat, poor nutrition, and chronic debilitating diseases, they are more likely to develop decubiti. Extended treatment and care are often necessary.

SUMMARY

Skin disorders increase with age, but rarely cause death if identified and treated early. Skin problems are usually preventable by a) avoiding over-exposure to the sun; b) maintaining an adequate diet and fluid intake; c) keeping the body clean; and d) avoiding local irritations or trauma.

BIBLIOGRAPHY

Books

Conrad, Adolph H. Jr. Dermatologic disorders. In Steinberg, Franz U., ed., *Cowdry's the Care of the Geriatric Patient,* 5th ed. St. Louis: Mosby, 1976.

Selmanowitz, Victor J., Rizer, Ronald L. and Orentreich, Norman. Aging of the skin and its appendages. In Finch, Caleb E. and Hayflick, Leonard, eds., *Handbook of the Biology of Aging.* New York: Van Nostrand Reinhold, 1977.

Periodicals

Carlsen, R. A. Aging skin: understanding the inevitable. *Geriatrics 30:*51, 1975.

Knox, J. M. Common sense care for the aging skin. *Geriatrics 30:*59, 1975.

Ogawa, C. M. Degenerative skin disorders: toll of age and sun. *Geriatrics 30:*65, 1975.

Spencer, S. K. and Kierland, R. R. The aging skin: problems and their causes. *Geriatrics 24:*81, 1970.

Unit 4

The Musculo-skeletal System

One of the most stressful aspects of older age is the increasing probability of major changes in life style, especially changes that are indicative of impending dependency. Independence is a strong cultural value in our society, while dependency is usually viewed as extremely undesirable. Studies show that older people list the fear of dependency as very high among their concerns about growing older.

Dependency at any age, but particularly in older age, often results from a decrement in physical mobility which produces an increasing inability to cope effectively with the necessary tasks of independent living. Mobility changes are most specifically the result of aging in the musculoskeletal system. Although its importance is not always fully appreciated, the musculoskeletal system allows for an amazing variety of body movements, ranging from movements of the entire body to those of very small parts of the body, and from slow movements to very fast and highly precise movements. Such a wide range of mobility options is necessary to cope with varied and complex life situations. Loss of individual mobility results ultimately in dependency on others.

Muscles act by contraction and relaxation. Normally, when one group of muscles contracts, an opposite or antagonistic muscle group relaxes. Muscles thus act on the bones of the skeleton to create an efficient leverage system for pulling, pushing, and lifting. Body movement is made possible by the interrelationship among the bony skeleton, the various muscles of the body, and the nervous system.

23

THE SKELETON

Components

The skeleton provides the supporting framework of the body. In the human it consists of more than 200 different bones. Basic components of the skeletal system include:

- The skull (enclosing and protecting the brain).
- The vertebral column, or backbone (a chain of 33 vertebrae enclosing the spinal cord).

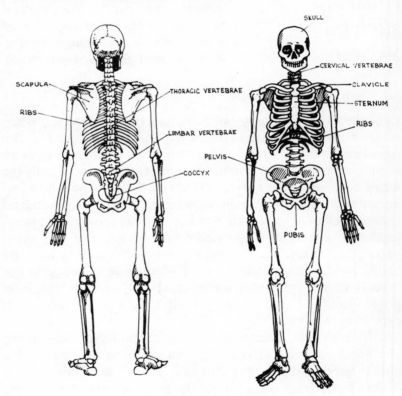

Figure 2. The skeleton, posterior and anterior views.

- Twelve pairs of ribs.
- The shoulder girdle (including the *scapula* or shoulder blade, and the *clavicle,* or collar bone).
- The upper extremities (arms), which are attached to the shoulder girdle.
- The breastbone (*sternum*), which is attached to the ribs.
- The lower extremities (legs), which are attached to the pelvic girdle.

Besides bone, the hard framework of the body, the skeletal system includes a) *cartilage,* a nonvascular connective tissue (often called gristle) which connects and supports various structures of the body; and b) *ligaments,* or bands of tough, fibrous yet flexible connective tissue which bind the bones together.

Functions of the Skeletal System

The major functions of the skeletal system are to:

1. Protect and support the organ systems of the body.
2. Provide places for attachments of muscles, tendons, and ligaments.
3. Serve as a site for the manufacture of blood cells (in bone marrow).
4. Serve as a storage depot for reserve calcium supply in the body.
5. Act in conjunction with the voluntary muscles as a leverage system for pushing, pulling, and lifting.

MUSCLES

Types of Muscles

There are three specific types of muscle tissue in the human body: smooth, striated, and cardiac.

● *Smooth muscle,* so named because of its appearance, is mostly under the control of the autonomic (automatic) nervous system and usually acts without conscious thought directed to the activity. For example, it is not necessary to command the smooth musculature of the digestive tract to begin digesting food. Digestion occurs without our conscious attention, although thoughts and emotions certainly influence the process. Action of smooth muscle typically tends to be slow, sustained, and often rhythmical.

Smooth muscle tissue is found principally in the a) walls of the digestive tract; b) trachea (windpipe) and bronchi; c) urinary bladder and gallbladder; d) ducts of the urinary and genital organs; e) walls of the blood vessels; f) spleen; g) iris of the eye; and h) hair follicles of the skin.

● *Striated muscle tissue,* sometimes referred to as striped muscle because of its appearance, constitutes the voluntary muscles of the body whose actions we consciously will or direct. Striated muscle is primarily stimulated by the cerebrospinal nerves rather than by the autonomic nervous system.

Muscles attached directly to the skeleton are striated muscle. In some cases, skeletal muscles are attached directly to bones; in other cases, a band of dense, fibrous tissue (tendon) connects skeletal muscle to the bones. Ligaments are bands of dense fibrous connective tissue connecting bones to other bones.

In addition to constituting skeletal muscles, striated muscle is also found in the a) tongue; b) soft palate; c) scalp; d) pharynx and upper part of the esophagus; and e) extrinsic eye muscles.

● *Cardiac muscle* is a special kind of muscle tissue found only in the heart. Stimulation of cardiac muscle is through the autonomic nervous system and action is principally (but not exclusively) involuntary, automatic, and rhythmic.

Characteristics of Muscle

Muscle tissue has at least four special characteristics:

1. Contractility, the ability to contract and become shorter.

2. Extensibility, the ability to stretch and become longer.

3. Elasticity, the ability to regain its original shape after having been stretched or contracted.

4. Irritability, or the ability to respond to stimulation. The usual stimulus for muscle action is a nerve impulse, but other stimuli such as electric shock, an irritating chemical, or a mechanical stimulus also produce muscle reactions.

Muscle tone, vitally important in physical fitness and health maintenance, is dependent upon these special properties of normal muscle tissue.

Muscle Function

Muscle movements have traditionally been classified as *voluntary* or *involuntary,* the former implying conscious control and the latter implying automatic or reflexive control. As already indicated, the difference between conscious and automatic control of movement is not very definite and precise. Recent research has demonstrated that some behaviors traditionally considered to be involuntary can be brought at least partially under voluntary control by using conditioning and biofeedback techniques. These behaviors include digestive processes, blood pressure, and heart rate. Thus, rigid distinctions between voluntary and involuntary functions are somewhat questionable. There is still much to be learned in this area and undoubtedly many more contributions and applications to the field of aging to be made.

However, to better understand the basic principles of muscle functioning in the human body, we shall distinguish between those activities primarily under voluntary control and those primarily under involuntary control.

Muscle activities primarily under voluntary control include a) maintenance of posture; and b) the majority of visible movements, such as facial expressions, locomotion, chewing, and manipulation of objects.

Muscle activities primarily under involuntary control include a) propulsion of material through the body, as for example, blood and food; b) expulsion of stored substances, such as bile from the gallbladder, feces from the intestinal tract, and urine from the kidneys and bladder (although the latter two are capable of conscious control most of the time); c) muscular regulation of size of body openings, such as the anus and the urethral opening; d) muscular regulation of the diameter of tubes such as blood vessels and bronchioles in the lungs.

Age-RelatedMusculoskeletal Changes

Atrophy of Muscles

Maximum muscular strength is usually attained by age 25 or 30. After that, there is a gradual decrease in the number of active muscle fibers in the body and in the bulk of muscle fibers. The resulting reduction in the size of muscles is referred to as *atrophy* or "wasting" of the muscles. (Anyone who has had an arm or leg encased in a cast for a few weeks has probably been surprised at the dramatic muscle atrophy observed when the cast is finally removed.) Disuse at any age very quickly produces atrophy in normal muscles. The aging process apparently produces atrophy also, but much more slowly. Older persons may be expected to have less muscle strength, to move more slowly, and to have a decreased capacity for sustained muscular contraction.

Loss of Muscle Elasticity

Muscles become less elastic and therefore less flexible with age. This, combined with age-related changes in skeletal joints, contributes to stiffness and possible immobility.

Because smooth muscles appear to be less affected by age

than skeletal muscles, they do not seem to be significantly impaired in older age except by accident or disease.

Recent research indicates that muscular changes (especially atrophy) are much less marked in individuals who remain physically active into old age. A survey of available research reports on "normal aging" shows that physical fitness resulting from regular, systematic exercise (not sporadic weekend endurance contests) and proper nutrition appear to be two of the best ways to offset many of the aches, pains, and mobility limitations of older age (16).

Osteoporosis, Kyphosis, and Scoliosis

One of the most significant age-related changes in bones is a *loss of bone mass*. As aging progresses, bones become more porous or less dense (osteoporosis). Osteoporosis is more common in women than in men and is likely to become apparent in the middle years of life (over 50). Although no one factor has been pinpointed as the definitive cause, possible causal factors are a) calcium deficiency due to bone resorption with age; b) possible age-related disturbances in protein metabolism; c) lack of regular and systematic exercise; and d) decrease in estrogen, often associated with the postmenopausal years.

Osteoporosis results in skeletal instability caused by the porous bones. Such bones are not capable of adequately supporting the body and are easily broken. Fractures are common and are a leading cause of disability in the elderly. Statistically, the most frequent types of fractures associated with osteoporosis are vertebral fractures. These often go undetected since small fractures of the vertebrae can occur without much pain being felt. Even simple activities such as coughing or sneezing can cause fractures in osteoporotic bones. These small vertebral fractures undoubtedly contribute to poor posture and to chronic back pain.

Osteoporosis may also alter back alignment, causing the characteristic bent or stooped posture of many older persons.

The "hump-backed" or flexed posture usually resulting from osteoporotic changes is called *kyphosis,* and S-shaped curvature of the spine is called *scoliosis.* Both are relatively common phenomena among the aged population. Kyphosis and scoliosis interfere with stability and balance, and thus may impede locomotion. A wide-stance or waddling gait is adopted as an attempt to change the center of gravity and offset alignment difficulties created by bone and muscle changes.

Back Pain

Back pain usually accompanies age-related changes in the vertebral discs of the spinal column. Normally the vertebrae are separated by discs that act as shock absorbers in the vertebral column. With age the discs may become dehydrated and less compressible, producing diminished flexibility and misalignment. In some instances the discs become compressed, leading to improperly separated vertebrae.

Postural Changes

Changes that take place in body musculature   and in the ligaments, tendons, and bones of the skeleton, especially those in the vertebral column, produce postural modifications characterized by bent or stooped body flexion. Poor posture adversely affects the functioning of other organ systems of the body and thus adds yet another handicap to the aging body's already limited ability to cope and adapt effectively.

Changes in Mobility

General mobility is impaired to some degree by connective tissue changes associated with age. Connective tissue is distributed throughout the body and serves to bind parts together and to support body structures. With age, connective tissue becomes less flexible, even calcified in some instances, and thereby contributes to decreased body flexibility.

Implications of Age-Related Musculoskeletal Changes

Functioning of Body Systems

Aging in muscles and bones also has these significant effects on the efficiency of other organs or organ systems:

1. Sharpness of vision decreases with age, partially because of weakening of the small muscles attached to the lens, the focusing element of the eye.

2. Skeletal and muscular changes associated with age affect the respiratory system when skeletal kyphosis (hunchback) reduces overall volume of the lungs, while loss of muscle strength affects breathing. Age-related changes in both bone and muscle contribute to reduced reserve capacity in the respiratory system.

3. Alterations in the musculature of the gastrointestinal tract and the urinary system produce changes in the ability to digest food and to regulate defecation and urination. The embarrassment of partial or complete incontinence often has a severely deleterious effect on self-confidence and feelings of self-esteem.

4. Muscles are one site of glycogen storage. Reduction in muscle mass results in reduced capacity to store glycogen, which is derived from carbohydrates and released when necessary to furnish quick energy in emergency situations. Thus, older people react more slowly to emergency situations.

Work and Play

Physical activities need to be paced more carefully to compensate for slower movements and decrease in strength and stamina. The concept of *pacing* suggests that each individual should do things in his/her own way and in his/her own time as much as possible. Pacing makes the difference between well-executed, competent performance and disorganized, inept efforts that culminate in frustration for all involved.

Environment

In planning programs and activities for older age groups, it is especially important to allow for periodic "stretch" breaks. Sitting for long periods of time can result in painful joint stiffness which lessens concentration on the activity or program being presented.

In the home, furniture should accommodate the older person's less flexible muscular and skeletal systems. Low, overstuffed chairs without arms, for example, make it difficult to rise and at the same time maintain balance. Protruding furniture legs increase the probability of accidents, as do scatter rugs, waxed floors, and water or food spilled on the floor. Poorly illuminated rooms and small house pets may also be environmental hazards.

In general, the home should be arranged so that accident hazards are reduced and safety devices increased.

Age-Related Disorders of the Musculoskeletal System

Muscle Cramps

A distressing disorder that increases with advancing age is muscle cramps. They frequently occur at night following periods of extreme physical activity. They are painful and involuntary, and commonly affect the thigh, calf, foot, hip, or hand. The cause is not known and persons who are otherwise normal may experience these symptoms.

Restless Legs

Restless legs, or a constant moving of the legs, sometimes occurs in elderly persons who suffer from *paresthesia,* which is a distorted sense of crawling, tingling, or burning of the skin.

Muscular Weakness and Paralysis

Emotional disorders, worry, anxiety, or stress can result in muscle tension and lack of complete muscle relaxation even during sleep or rest. Common complaints include pain in the joints and head, and general muscle soreness.

Myasthenia Gravis

Myasthenia gravis is a progressive chronic disease in which there is a defect in the impulses transmitted from nerves to the muscle cell. It is found particularly in men over 60 years of age and is characterized by extreme muscle weakness. Symptoms include ptosis (sagging) of the eyelids, double vision, difficulty in breathing and in swallowing, generalized weakness, fatigue, and prostration. Death may ensue.

Other Muscle Disorders

Other muscle problems experienced by the elderly may be caused by a variety of factors such as decreased potassium level in the body, hyperthyroidism, diseases of the connective tissue, malnutrition, diabetes, or arteriosclerosis.

Arthritis

Arthritis affects over 17 million Americans and is prevalent among the elderly. The term arthritis refers to joint inflammation, but there are types of arthritis that involve the tendons and muscles as well. A frequently heard complaint of older persons —"Oh, my arthritis (or rheumatism),"—usually refers to almost any ache or pain.

Degenerative arthritis.   The most common form of arthritis in people after age 50 is degenerative or *osteoarthritis.* Sixty percent of persons over 60 have been estimated to show some evidence of this disease. The causes are multiple and include heredity, obesity, living environment, and wear and tear on the joints. This chronic disease affects the movable joints and is noninflammatory. It involves the degeneration of the articular cartilage of the joints, displacing it with new bone formation. Multiple joints may be affected, but it is more commonly seen in one particular site. Weight-bearing joints such as hips and knees, as well as joints of the spine, shoulders, and fingers are often affected. Symptoms are rare early in the disease, but in its later stages pain, stiffness upon rising, and crepitation (creaking joints) are usual. Restriction of joint motion results from disuse caused by pain, spasms, and the degenerative changes occurring within the joint. This disease progresses gradually without periods of remission.

Rheumatoid arthritis. In contrast to degenerative arthritis, rheumatoid arthritis can involve the connective tissue of the entire body, but is manifested more specifically in the joints. This disease usually occurs between ages 20 and 60, although appearance after 60 is not uncommon. Onset may be sudden in older persons and periods of remission are typical. The small joints of the hands and feet are frequently affected, resulting in deformity and disability. In general, it is more disabling than degenerative arthritis.

Gout

Gout is a disease of faulty metabolism in which there is an increase in uric acid in the blood and deposition of uric acid crystals in the joints. The cause is not known, although there seems to be a familial tendency to develop gout. Any joint may be affected, but the big toe is a common site. Attacks are sudden and joint pain is excruciating, lasting from five to eight days, during which time victims become incapacitated. The disease is self-limiting, but after repeated acute attacks chronic gout is likely. Joints are sometimes left deformed, painful, and permanently disabled.

Bursitis

In the joints where tendons or muscles pass over bones are *bursas* or pockets containing small amounts of fluid. Infection, calcium deposits, or trauma cause bursas to become inflamed and the amount of fluid in them to increase, resulting in pain upon movement of the joint. The most commonly affected sites are the shoulder and the elbow. Response to treatment is slow and the disease can become chronic.

Fractures

The elderly have a high incidence of fractures, and resulting disabilities of the back and lower limbs are a leading cause of restricted activity in this age group. A variety of factors predispose the older person to fracture. Among these are poor nutrition, muscle weakness, disturbances in balance, reduced reaction time, osteoporosis, mental confusion, limited eyesight, and a host of physical diseases.

A serious fracture for older persons is fracture of the hip. Sometimes these fractures are due to falls or other accidents, but it is possible that in some instances the osteoporotic hip joint breaks or "gives way," causing the person to fall. Fractures and their resultant complications are a common cause of traumatic death for persons over 75. New treatment techniques, however, permit rehabilitation and return to a meaningful life for numerous persons who formerly might have died from prolonged immobility or confinement to bed. Unfortunately, many elderly are uninformed or misinformed about recent treatment procedures that permit ambulation and a return to independence in a relatively short time. It is imperative that family, friends, and medical personnel provide older people with reassurance, support, and accurate factual information about their physical condition and the prospects for rehabilitation following fractures. Grab rails on bathtubs or within reach of toilets, railings on stairs, and supportive furniture help to reduce the possibility of unexpected falls. Most falls occur in the home, so attention should be directed to "accident proofing" the day-to-day environment. Although home arrangement ought to minimize stressful efforts such as reaching, bending, climbing or stooping, physical activity in moderation is very desirable and provides beneficial exercise in conjunction with doing one's daily household tasks.

Offsetting the Effects of Aging

In order to minimize the effects of age-related changes in muscle and bone the older person should a) be more attentive to maintaining proper posture and muscle tone; b) keep a proper weight; and c) engage in regular and systematic exercise. Everyone over 30 should have a physical examination before embarking on an exercise or fitness program. Physical fitness and firm muscle tone can at least partially offset the detrimental effects of musculoskeletal changes known to be associated with advancing age. Since mobility equals independence, it is vitally important.

BIBLIOGRAPHY
Books

Avioli, Louis V. Aging, bone, and osteoporosis. In Steinberg, Franz, ed., *Cowdry's the Care of the Geriatric Patient,* 5th ed. St. Louis: Mosby, 1976.

Brunner, Lillian S. and Suddarth, Doris S. *Textbook of Medical Surgical Nursing,* 3rd ed. Philadelphia: Lippincott, 1975.

Exton-Smith, A. N. Musculoskeletal system. In Brocklehurst, J. C., ed., *Textbook of Geriatric Medicine and Gerontology.* Edinburgh and London: Churchill Livingstone, 1973.

Gutman, E. Muscle. In Finch, Caleb E. and Hayflick, Leonard, eds., *Handbook of the Biology of Aging.* New York: Van Nostrand Reinhold, 1977.

Hartenstein, Roy. *Human Anatomy and Physiology.* New York: Van Nostrand, 1976.

Steen, Edwin B. and Montagu, Ashley. *Anatomy and Physiology,* Vol. 1. New York: Barnes and Noble, 1959.

Tokay, Elbert. *Fundamentals of Physiology.* rev. ed. New York: Barnes and Noble, 1972.

Periodicals

Azar, Gordon and Lawton, A. H. Gait and stepping as factors in the frequent falls of elderly women. *Gerontologist 4:*83, 1964.

Bandilla, K. K. Back pain: osteoarthritis. *Journal of the American Geriatric Society 25:*62, 1977.

Gaskowitz, Roland W. Osteoarthritis: a new look at an old disease. *Geriatrics 28:*121, 1973.

Hester, Raymond B. and Bennett, Claude J. Rheumatoid arthritis: an immune complex disease. *Geriatrics 28:*84, 1973.

Horenstein, S. Managing gait disorders. *Geriatrics 29:*86, 1974.

Kolodny, A. L. and Klipper, A. R. Bone and joint diseases in the elderly. *Hospital Practitioner 11:*91, 1976.

Leeming, J. T. Skeletal disease in the elderly. *British Journal of Medicine 4:*472, 1973.

McBeath, A. A. The aging skeleton, osteoporosis and degenerative arthritis. *Postgraduate Medicine 57:*171, 1975.

Rundle, A. T. and Dollimore, J. Age-related bone change. *Journal of Mental Deficiency Research 20:*55, 1976.

Smith, R. O., Walton, R. J. and Woods, C. G. Osteoporosis of aging. *Lancet 1:*40, 1976.

Steinberg, Franz. Gait disorders in the aged. *Journal of the American Geriatric Society 20:*537, 1972.

Webster, S. G. P., Leeming, J. T. and Wilkinson, E. M. The causes of osteomalacia in the elderly. *Age and Ageing 5:*119, 1976.

Unit 5

The Nervous System

The nervous system, probably the most complicated system in the body, coordinates and integrates all bodily activities. Adaptive behavior is dependent upon a) receiving accurate information from both external and internal (body) environments, b) processing and interpreting such information appropriately, and c) responding to new information in an adaptive and life-sustaining manner.

The crucial link to the world in which we live is a complex three-unit chain: *receptors* to receive information; *nervous system* to process and interpret information; and *effectors* to act on information.

Receptors are nerve endings that respond to stimuli impinging on them. In lower animals a single receptor may be sensitive to all stimulation, but in humans receptors have become highly specialized and react adequately only to very specific stimulation. For example, the specialized receptors for vision, hearing, taste, touch, and smell respond appropriately only to visual, auditory, taste, touch, and smell stimuli respectively.

Specialized receptors in humans are grouped into three types:

● *Exteroceptors* are specialized receptors located on or near the surface of the body to receive information from the external world. Examples are the receptors for the "special senses"; i.e., vision, hearing, taste, touch, and smell.

● *Interoceptors* are specialized receptors located inside the organism; they receive information about the internal environment of the body. Receptors in the viscera or internal organs supply information about sensations of pain, hunger, nausea, and so forth. Such internal information is vital, although we sometimes forget or underplay its significance for general health and well-being. For instance, it is important to know when the appendix becomes inflamed, and pain localized in the lower right side provides a significant clue.

● *Proprioceptors* are specialized receptors located in muscles, tendons, and joints; they give one continuous information about one's body position in space. To test this, close your eyes and extend your right arm horizontally. You are aware of the position of the arm solely because of "muscle information" you receive from the proprioceptors.

The degree of specialization found in human receptors makes for a wide range of sensitivity to many different kinds of stimuli and allows for continuous awareness of conditions in both internal and external environments. Such a monitoring system provides fast, constant, up-to-date information about life status of the moment.

The nervous system is the second link in the chain and is composed of the following:

● *Central nervous system* (CNS), including the brain and the spinal cord.

● *Peripheral nervous system* (PNS), including the somatic nervous system ("body nerves").

● *Autonomic nervous system* (ANS) with its two divisions, parasympathetic and sympathetic.

The basic functional unit of the nervous system is the *neuron,* or nerve cell. The nervous system receives sensory information through the various receptors, transmits it throughout the system by way of nerves and nerve impulses, interprets the information in the brain and to a lesser extent in the spinal cord, and makes a decision as to action. If action is necessary, a message is sent to the effectors directly responsible for producing the desired action.

Effectors are nerve endings in muscles, glands, and organs that act to produce change. If you are attempting to cross the street and you see a car coming, this information is transmitted to your brain where the decision is made as to whether you should cross, wait until the car passes, walk, run, or whatever. Such decisions depend upon your acquired knowledge of cars and speed factors, your fear of being hurt, how fast you can move, and so on. Once a decision is made, muscles and glands are sent the appropriate messages and action takes place. This explanation is obviously far too simplistic as many additional systems of the body are involved in such behavior, but it allows for some understanding of the complexity and speed of decision-making as well as consequent behaviors that are made possible by means of the receptor-nervous system-effector circuit.

CENTRAL NERVOUS SYSTEM

The central nervous system (CNS) includes the brain and the spinal cord. Both are enclosed by bony structures and cushioned by cerebrospinal fluid which completely surrounds them.

Brain

The human brain represents the highest known form of development in the evolutionary scale. Some functions of the brain are:

1. To integrate and regulate the body's activities.
2. To initiate all the voluntary acts of behavior.
3. To serve as the locus for learning, memory, thought, reasoning, and other complex mental activity.
4. To serve as the center for sensations and consciousness (awareness).
5. To act as the locus of emotions and drives.

The brain may be subdivided into three principal parts: the brain stem, the cerebellum, and the cerebrum.

Brain stem.   The brain stem includes all the brain's structures other than cerebrum and cerebellum; specifically, the medulla oblongata, pons, midbrain, and diencephalon.

● The *medulla oblongata* is the lowermost part of the brain (at the base of the skull) and is continuous with the spinal cord. Two important functions of the medulla are a) to serve as the connecting pathway between ascending and descending nerve fibers linking brain and spinal cord; and b) to mediate and control certain vital activities such as heartbeat, swallowing, respiration rate, and blood flow. It is an extremely vital center and for this reason a hard blow to the base of the brain may be fatal if it interrupts life-sustaining medullary-mediated activities.

● The *pons* is a part of the brain stem situated directly above the medulla. Like the medulla oblongata, it acts as a major relay center for ascending and descending nerve impulses, and is the site of a number of large nuclei (collections of nerve cells) for several of the cranial nerves.

● The *midbrain,* situated above the pons, is significant primarily because of its relay functions. It includes several large nuclei, plays a part in the maintenance of balance and equilibrium, and serves as a major reflex center for vision and hearing.

● Two significant structures in the *diencephalon* are the *thalamus* and the *hypothalamus.* The diencephalon is sometimes included as part of the cerebrum since it is anatomically situated immediately below the cerebrum, but in our classification system it represents the uppermost part of the brain stem. The principal function of the thalamus is to serve as a major relay center between the cerebral cortex and lower nervous system components. A principal function of the hypothalamus is to regulate body temperature. The diencephalon also serves as a reflex center and acts in conjunction with the autonomic nervous system, and plays a significant role in the mediation of emotional behavior.

Cerebellum. The cerebellum is located posterior to the medulla and pons. Functions of the cerebellum are primarily:

1. Maintenance of muscle tone, posture, and equilibrium.
2. Coordination of voluntary muscle movements (skilled acts).

It is a highly significant integrative center for voluntary bodily activity and for coordination of certain reflexive behaviors related to body position and movement.

Cerebrum. The two hemispheres of the cerebrum are connected by a broad band of fibers, the *corpus callosum.* The cortex (surface) of the brain has many folds and furrows. Such a convoluted surface makes it possible to include a large mass of brain tissue within the relatively small human head.

Localized areas on the cortex that receive impulses from specific receptors are a) visual area, located in the occipital lobe; b) auditory area, located in the temporal lobe; c) sensory area (touch, pressure, temperature), located in the parietal lobe; d) motor area (control over skeletal muscles), between the frontal and parietal lobes; and e) association areas located in the frontal lobe and part of the parietal and temporal lobes (presumed to control speech, thought, learning, memory, and other intellectual behaviors). Essentially, the left half of the brain controls the right half of the body and the right half of the brain controls the left half of the body.

Spinal Cord

The spinal cord is located within the vertebral canal of the spinal column. At the "top" it is continuous with the medulla; at the "bottom" it tapers off in the region of the "tailbone" at the base of the spine. Thirty-one pairs of nerves emerge from the spinal cord, one pair at each spinal segment. Nerves leaving the cord at the base become the *cauda equina* (translated as "horse's tail" since this is what they resemble).

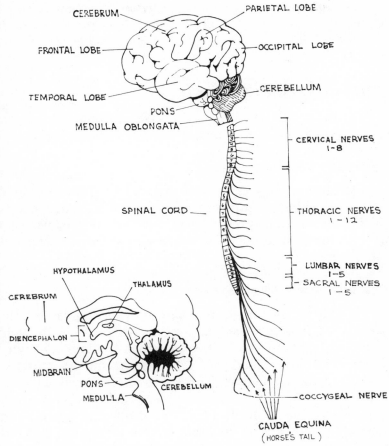

Figure 3. Central nervous system and cross section of the human brain.

The basic functions of the spinal cord are:

1. To serve as a conducting pathway to and from the brain and the rest of the nervous system.

2. To act as a reflex center since some simple reflexes can be controlled at spinal cord level. The knee jerk reflex is an example of a simple reflex controlled primarily at the spinal cord

level. In humans, however, most behavior is infinitely more complicated and usually involves nerves and muscles on both sides of the body as well as different spinal cord levels and the brain.

PERIPHERAL NERVOUS SYSTEM

The peripheral nervous system (PNS) includes the somatic nervous system and the automatic nervous system (ANS).

The Somatic Nervous System

The somatic nervous system includes 12 pairs of cranial nerves connecting sensory organs, 31 pairs of spinal nerves bringing information into the spinal cord and carrying messages out from the cord to the effectors, as well as various interconnecting nerves.

The Autonomic Nervous System

Possibly the more important part of the peripheral nervous system is the *autonomic nervous system* (ANS). The autonomic nervous system, through its two principal divisions, the sympathetic and parasympathetic, activates the smooth muscles, glands, and cardiac muscle. These structures control activities essential to life. For example, the heart, blood vessels, respiratory organs, kidneys, bladder, reproductive organs, and endocrine glands are all activated by the autonomic nervous system. It has two divisions—the parasympathetic division and the sympathetic division.

The Parasympathetic Division.   This division of the ANS functions when the body is relatively quiescent or at rest. It tends to have an individual and specific effect on body organs rather than acting on the body as a whole. It controls in part such activities as digestion, constriction of the pupils of the eyes, slowing down of the heart, and increased storage of glycogen by the liver.

The Sympathetic Division.   This division usually opposes the parasympathetic system in function, thus maintaining balanced activity in the body. It is considered to be the arousal system in the body—the emergency system for fast mobilization and quick release of energy. Activation of the sympathetic division affects the entire body rather than just individual organs. Sympathetic control increases heart rate, decreases gastric motility so that blood may be shunted to the muscles for immediate use, dilates pupils, temporarily stops metabolic body storage activities, and energizes the entire organism.

The autonomic nervous system (ANS) is entirely motor; that is, it has some control over all the effector organs of the body except voluntary muscles. The ANS is, in turn, controlled to some extent by the higher brain centers, particularly the medulla, hypothalamus, and cerebral cortex.

Normally, homeostatic equilibrium is maintained effectively by the ANS in conjunction with other organ systems, and the reciprocal relationship between its parasympathetic and sympathetic divisions generally prevents extremes in body regulatory activities. In a fear situation, for instance, one of the most obvious bodily changes is increase in heart rate (sympathetic influence). It would not be physiologically appropriate for an increased heart rate to continue indefinitely but, due to parasympathetic intervention following sympathetic activation, heart rate usually returns to normal within a short time after excitation.

The autonomic nervous system keeps us reacting appropriately to ongoing change in the environment without having to involve the highest brain centers in constant reasoning, intuitive thought, and decisionmaking over every bit of stimulation impacting on us.

Age-Related Changes in the Nervous System

Certain problems arise in attempting to generalize about the significance of the aging process as it affects the nervous system. Because of difficulties involved in obtaining data, much basic research has emphasized the pathological rather than the normal processes of aging. Also, a substantial amount of the available information is based primarily on estimates of age-related change, and a number of the estimates derive from animal research. The process of human aging is highly individualized and individual physiological, psychological, and social life experiences make for enormous variability among people of the same chronological age. In spite of these difficulties, certain basic age-related changes appear consistently even though the implications for behavior are not always clear.

Researchers have been especially interested in how the nervous system ages because nerve cells are nonreplenishing tissues of the body; that is, once nerve cells die, others are not regenerated to take their place. Red blood cells, for instance, live only about 120 days but new cells are constantly being manufactured so that the total supply is not diminished in any significant manner. Consequently, the age of blood cells is variable. Nerve cells, though, denote the true age of the organism since they are present at birth and when they die, they are not replaced.

Changes in Nerve Cells

1. It sounds rather dramatic to say that, according to most estimates (and they are only estimates), we lose thousands of brain cells daily after age 30. Fortunately, we have a very large number of nerve cells (neurons) to begin with, far more than we can ever use, so this estimated loss, if indeed it does occur, does not appear to impair behavior appreciably.

2. The cells of the non-nervous or supporting tissue of the brain and spinal cord increase with age.

3. In animals, older nerve cells change form so that the nucleus of the cell and its cytoplasm (the surrounding material), which once looked very different, become virtually indistinguishable. These changes are most apparent in the large

cells of the cerebellum and the cerebral cortex. Whether this affects mental functioning, especially memory loss, as has been suggested, is open to question at this time.

4. Appearance of a brownish pigment (lipofuscin) in nerve cells occurs consistently in older individuals. Lipofuscin also accumulates in cardiac muscle, skeletal muscle, smooth muscle, thymus, pancreas, adrenals, liver, spleen, and parts of the sperm ducts. Lipofuscin is thought by some to be related to senility, but again evidence is not clear. Some suggest that lipofuscin may be dependent upon cell activity in that the more active ("normal") the cell, the less the possibility that lipofuscin will accumulate.

5. Generally, biochemical activity lessens with age, particularly in very old age. Such decrease in brain biochemical activity is assumed to be associated with both the age-related decrease in the number of active neurons in the nervous system and the corresponding increase in numbers of nonmetabolically active cells (lipofuscin pigmented cells and supporting tissue cells).

6. Similarly, age-related change may occur in overall cerebral blood flow and oxygen use. A striking characterisic of nerve cells is that they are especially sensitive to a lack of oxygen. Research indicates that both blood circulation in the brain and the utilization of oxygen are reduced gradually and progressively after adolescence. Cerebral arteriosclerosis, so frequently seen in older persons, could well result in decreased blood flow or other cardiovascular deterioration. Involvement of the total circulatory system would be expected to have greater behavioral consequences than a limited, local circulatory change.

The aging brain is assumed by many to be hypoxic (oxygen deficient) because less oxygen is available in the presence of arteriosclerosis and the accumulation of pigments and metabolically inert supporting cells. Hypoxia (lack of adequate oxygen) may produce insomnia, irritability, memory difficulty, and visual-motor impairment. Experiments using hyperbaric oxygen (pure oxygen) chambers have demonstrated at least transient behavioral and performance improvement in older persons. A reasonable conclusion appears to be that intermittent hyperoxygenation can improve the thinking and reasoning abilities of older people suffering from arteriosclerosis, although it does not seem to reverse or slow the underlying degenerative process (17). More basic research is needed in this area.

Changes in Transmission Efficiency

If the central nervous system is viewed as a transmitting and receiving center where messages are transmitted over very complex circuits from the sensory organs to the brain, from the brain back to the sensory effectors and organs, and from one part of the brain to another, the necessity for efficiency in the sending, transmitting, and receiving parts of the system is apparent.

Several factors possibly affect transmission efficiency in older persons: a) the decreased numbers of functional nerve cells perhaps reduce the strength of the message being transmitted; b) fewer nerve cells result in more space to cross and the coherence of the message may be disrupted, or random background noise (neural noise) could interfere with the clarity of the message; or c) the motor part of the older cerebral cortex may continue to respond for a time after stimulation ceases and such aftereffects tend to blur or interfere with subsequent incoming messages. This could account for the increased time older people usually need to perform simple tasks as well as for their poorer retention and increased susceptibility to distraction in learning and memory tasks.

Changes in Brain Wave Patterns

Brain wave patterns (EEG), which reflect the electrical activity of the brain, change with age. Older persons' EEG patterns are likely to be slower and may resemble the EEG pattern of a child in the early developmental years. Individual differences in EEG patterns increase with age, though. These minor age-related changes in EEGs of healthy older people seem to have no apparent functional correlation with learning, memory, perception, or sensorimotor behaviors.

Changes in Sleep Patterns

Sleep patterns change with age. By age 50 the stage of deep sleep declines to about 50 percent of what it was at age 20. Quality of sleep begins to change in the 40s with more awakenings and more time awake as we grow older. Such sleep-wake patterns are common, but actual behavioral implications of age-related changes in sleep are not yet consistent or clear enough to formulate reliable generalizations.

Changes in the Autonomic Nervous System

Age-related changes in the ANS seem to be basically related to slowness of functioning and to the prolonged recovery time required after activation. More research is needed in this area before adequate generalizations can be made. There is substantial controversy over whether people become more or less aroused and activated by the environment as they grow older and some evidence exists to support each point of view.

Judging from research data currently available, the nervous system may well be affected more by decremental aging in other systems of the body than by intrinsic changes in nervous tissue. Known nervous system changes associated with age could account at least partially for the increased slowness of behavior so characteristic of older age, but beyond that, there is too much individual variation to warrant responsible generalizations.

Age-Related Disorders of the Nervous System

Stroke (CVA)

Cerebrovascular accidents (CVA) or strokes are discussed in the section on the circulatory system (Unit 7). Additional discussion is not included here except to remind the reader that a CVA involves varying degrees of neurologic damage to the brain itself.

Senile Tremor

The cause of tremor is not always known, but hypotheses suggest that age-related destruction of some neurons releases other neurons from their inhibitory functions, resulting in involuntary movements or tremors. Senile tremor involves primarily the head, neck, and face, but may also affect the limbs. Head-nodding, head-shaking, rhythmic opening and shutting of the jaws, and more bizarre repetitive movements fall into this category.

Parkinson's Disease

More prevalent among men over 50 than among women, Parkinson's disease is also known as "shaking palsy" since the most obvious symptoms are tremor and muscular rigidity. The specific cause of this disease is usually unknown, but it may be related to deterioration in the integrating centers of the brain. Parkinsonian symptoms include a mask-like facial expression, a fine "pill-rolling" tremor beginning in the hands and fingers, muscle rigidity, drooling, difficulty in swallowing, increased susceptibility to falls, and emotional lability ("mood swings"). These specific symptoms plus other physical and psychological problems increase as the disease progresses. Persons with this illness need continued emotional support and understanding from those around them. Accurate diagnosis is necessary to differentiate true Parkinson's disease from the various tremors of advancing age. In recent years new drugs have been quite effective in treatment of this disease.

Herpes Zoster (Shingles)

A frequent and distressing disease often appearing for the first time in older age is herpes zoster—"shingles." Caused by an inflammation that attacks cutaneous nerves, it is an extremely painful disorder. Herpes zoster is a systemic infection caused by a virus,and is especially dangerous if it affects the eyes. The older debilitated person with shingles is likely to develop neuritis that may last for months and be very painful.

Trigeminal Neuralgia (Tic Douloureux)

Trigeminal neuralgia is common among the elderly, especially women, but rare in those under 50 years of age. Involvement of the trigeminal nerve in the face causes bursts of agonizing pain so fierce that subjects are hesitant to eat or even move for fear of aggravating it. Anxiety and apprehension usually accompany tic douloureux because of the intensity of the attacks. Both drugs and surgical intervention have been used with some success in the control of this chronic health problem.

Brain Tumor

Most brain tumors among the elderly are not primary lesions but result from the spread of cancer that originated in another body site. Symptoms vary and may include sensorimotor disturbances or personality changes. Brain tumors are not a significant problem among the older population.

BIBLIOGRAPHY

Books

Agate, John. *The Practice of Geriatrics,* 2nd ed. Springfield, Ill.: Charles C Thomas, 1970.

Bondareff, William. The neural basis of aging. In Birren, James E. and Schaie, K. Warner, eds., *Handbook of the Psychology of Aging.* New York: Van Nostrand Reinhold, 1977.

Brody, Harold and Vijayashanker, N. Anatomical changes in the nervous system. In Finch, Caleb E. and Hayflick, Leonard, eds., *Handbook of the Biology of Aging.* New York: Van Nostrand Reinhold, 1977.

Dayan, A. D. Central nervous system. In Brocklehurst, J. C., ed., *Textbook of Geriatric Medicine and Gerontology*. Edinburgh and London: Churchill Livingstone, 1973.

Frolkis, Vladimir V. Aging of the autonomic nervous system. In Birren, James E. and Schaie, K. Warner, eds., *Handbook of the Psychology of Aging*. New York: Van Nostrand Reinhold, 1977.

Hardin, William B. Neurologic aspects. In Steinberg, Franz, ed., *Cowdry's the Care of the Geriatric Patient,* 5th ed. St. Louis: Mosby, 1976.

Hodkinson, H. M. *An Outline of Geriatrics*. New York: Academic Press, 1975.

Puner, Morton. *To the Good Long Life*. New York: Universe, 1974.

Teyler, Timothy. *A Primer of Psychobiology*. San Francisco: Freeman, 1975.

Timiras, P. S., ed. *Developmental Physiology and Aging*. New York: Macmillan, 1972.

Tokay, Elbert. *Fundamentals of Physiology,* rev. ed. New York: Barnes and Noble, 1972.

Periodicals

Berlin, M. and Wallace, R. B. Aging and the central nervous system. *Experimental Aging Research 2:*125, 1976.

Hanley, T. "Neuronal fall-out" in the ageing brain; a critical review of the quantitative data. *Age and Ageing 3:*133, 1974.

Hasselkus, B. R. Aging and the human nervous system. *American Journal of Occupational Therapy 28:*16, 1974.

Heilman, K. M. Exploring the enigmas of frontal lobe dysfunction. *Geriatrics 31:*81, 1976.

Kent, S. Structural changes in the brain may short-circuit transfer of information. *Geriatrics 31:*128, 1976.

Kokmen, E., Bossemeyer, Jr., R. W. Barney, J. and Williams, W. J. Neurological manifestations of aging. *Journal of Gerontology 32:*411, 1977.

Semorajski, T. How the human brain responds to aging. *Journal of the American Geriatrics Society 24:*4, 1976.

Smith, B. H. and Sethi, P. K. Aging and the nervous system. *Geriatrics 30:*109, 1975.

Stein, D. B. and Firl, A. C. Brain damage and reorganization of function in old age. *Experimental Neurology 52:*156, 1976.

Unit 6

The Sensory Systems

All knowledge of the world in which we live comes to us through our sensory systems. To survive, we must constantly be aware of the environment and the changes taking place within it. We must also be able to interpret incoming information, to integrate it with knowledge about our body state at the moment, and to act upon it in an adaptive manner.

Adequate behavior, in fact life itself, depends upon the integrity of the receptor-nervous system-effector chain discussed in Unit 5. Inaccurate or partial information received in the nervous system may result in distorted or inappropriate behavior. Such behavior is particularly significant in older persons who are attempting to maintain independence and control in the face of the various decline factors and cumulating losses associated with advancing age. In older age, the amount and quality of sensory input are vital factors in adaptive and adjustive behavior. Various research and clinical data suggest that humans need both an adequate amount and an adequate variety of stimulation in order to remain mentally intact and in contact with the real world. The behavioral implications of sensory deprivation resulting from the aging process are intriguing and complex.

Sensory systems of major concern in the study of aging are visual (sight), auditory (hearing), gustatory (taste), tactile (touch), olfactory (smell), vestibular (balance), and kinesthetic ("muscle sense"). Each contributes a specific type of information necessary for continuing adaptation and adjustment.

Sensory changes tend to begin in the 40s or 50s with a gradual reduction in acuity or sharpness of discrimination, but do not appreciably limit behavior until about the 70s or 80s. For

53

example, it is common to observe a 40-year-old person holding a newspaper at arm's length due to the increasing farsightedness of middle age, but age-related poor vision may not curtail his/her driving until many years later. Having to hold a paper at arm's length may be a nuisance, but it doesn't limit behavior or change total life style as non-driving does. Being "without wheels" in our mobile society has far-reaching psychological and social consequences for many older persons. The best programs and services ever devised will be of little use if lack of transportation makes them inaccessible, as is often the case among the elderly.

It is not possible to predict individual behavioral capabilities or limitations by measuring the decrease in functioning of a given sensory system. First, there is significant variation among individuals in the rate of aging. Second, the degree of loss is variable from one organ system to another within a given individual. Third, humans have an amazing ability to adapt to and compensate for gradual changes. For some, compensation and adaptation to a large sensory loss may be so effective that his/her activities of daily living (ADL) are only minimally affected. For others, a minimal sensory loss will produce major changes in life style, and may even result in the individual becoming housebound or a functional invalid. If we could learn better ways to assist people in adapting to and compensating efficiently for gradual age-related changes, we could probably eliminate a number of the common problems that beset many of the elderly today as well as prolong their personal independence and self-maintenance. Fourth, some sensory systems are obviously more important in everyday functioning than others. We live primarily in a visual and auditory world and are, therefore, extremely dependent on the functional integrity of sight and hearing in dealing with day-to-day needs. Loss of smell, for instance, does not handicap an individual as much as the loss of vision.

One generalization that can be made safely about sensory

change and age is that, as we age, we need stronger stimuli to activate the sensory receptors, e.g., the lights need to be brighter, the sounds louder, and the smells stronger for the aging person to obtain the amount of information from the environment that is needed for effective action. This fact has enormous practical implications for creatively improving and manipulating environments in order to make them more supportive for older individuals.

VISION

The main structures in the eye are:
- The *sclera,* which is the outer layer of the eyeball, or the "white" of the eye.
- The *cornea,* which is the transparent sclera at the front of the eye (light rays enter the eye through the cornea).
- The *retina,* or inner layer, which contains rods and cones, the receptors for vision. Rods mediate dim light or night vision, while cones are responsible for day vision. Rods and cones are distributed differently on the retinal surface. Cones are clustered at the back of the retina in an area of maximal concentration called the *fovea,* and rods are located predominantly along the sides of the retina. To see an object most distinctly at night or under very low illumination, one should look slightly off to the side of the object rather than directly at it, as more rods will then be stimulated than cones. The human retina is estimated to contain about 125 million rods and 6 million cones. Approximately 50,000 cones are concentrated in the fovea, the area of sharpest and most distinct vision.
- The *iris,* a thin, colored, circular disc is suspended between the cornea and the lens. The opening at the center is the *pupil.* The color of the iris gives identifying color to the eyes and its function is to regulate the amount of light entering the eye through dilation (opening) and contraction (closing), actions which change pupil size. When illumination is low or dim, the pupil opening becomes large (dilated) allowing a maximum

amount of light to stimulate receptors. In bright light, pupils contract and the opening becomes smaller so that receptors will be stimulated but not damaged by intense light rays.

● The transparent crystalline *lens* focuses light rays so that they converge, or come to a point precisely on the part of retinal surface that will produce the sharpest vision. The relatively flexible lens, suspended in place behind the iris by ligaments and ciliary muscles, can flatten or bulge its shape as necessary. Changing lens shape to bring converging light rays to a focus directly on the retinal surface (the process of *accommodation*) allows for very sharp and precise vision at both near and far distances. In some people the shape of the eyeball or the shape of the lens brings light rays to a focus at a point beyond the retinal surface and results in hyperopia (farsightedness). Similarly, the shape of either the eyeball or the lens may produce myopia (nearsightedness) when light rays come to a focus at a point in front of the retinal surface rather than directly on it. *Astigmatism,* or irregularities in the curvature of the cornea or the lens, is another common visual problem. Hyperopia, myopia, and astigmatism can usually be corrected by prescription eyeglasses.

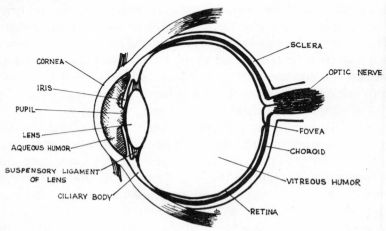

Figure 4. The eye.

● Inside the eye are fluids called the *aqueous humor* and the *vitreous humor.*

● At the back of the eyeball where the optic nerve leaves the eye is a *blind spot* as no receptors are present at this location.

Judging from the arrangement of eyes, humans evolved as predators. The eyes of predatory animals are usually close together in the front of the head, permitting excellent depth perception, while the eyes of prey animals (rabbit, deer) are usually spaced far apart and located more on the sides of the head in order to best detect movements (of predators) to the sides and behind them.

Age-Related Changes in Vision

Increase in Visual Threshold

The visual threshold increases with age. The most significant change in the visual system, or at least the change with the most implications for behavior, is that more light is needed to adequately stimulate visual receptors. Visual threshold refers to the minimum amount of light that will stimulate the rods or cones and trigger a nerve impulse to the brain, thereby registering visual information in the highest centers of the nervous system. A higher visual threshold means that older persons need greater illumination to obtain the maximum amount of visual information from the environment. This should always be taken into consideration in designing optimal living-working situations for middle-aged and older persons.

Decrease in Visual Acuity

Visual acuity (sharpness of vision) decreases with age. Visual acuity is poor in children, improves in young adulthood, and begins to decline gradually at about age 40. Changes in the lens, pupil size, composition of vitreous humor, and ability to shift from near to far vision all serve to decrease the sharpness of visual images as we grow older. To be useful to older persons, reading material should be printed in larger-than-usual type with a clear, distinct type face.

Decrease in Size of Pupil

Pupil size becomes slightly smaller with age. This means that less light enters the eye due to narrowing of the opening through which light rays pass. It is estimated that, because of reduced pupil size plus some yellowing of the lens with age, a 60-year-old person's retina receives only approximately 30 percent as much light as would reach the retina of a 20-year-old person.

Changes in the Lens

Lens changes in the aging have several effects on the efficiency of the visual system. These include:

"Yellow Filter Effect."   As aging occurs, the lens tends to become more yellow; this is the so-called "yellow filter effect." The amount of light entering the eye is thereby reduced and color perception may be affected. Older persons with distorted color perception are often able to discriminate between reds and yellows better than between blues, greens, and purples. Some institutions use color coding in attempts to modify behavior in therapeutically appropriate ways. For example, painting restroom doors a standard bright color (red) and dining room doors another color (yellow) may increase mobility and social interaction among nursing-home residents, as distinct color coding apparently makes space and place orientation easier and residents are more willing to move about. Color coding might well be used effectively in many other situations, such as in public buildings, transportation systems, or in housing areas.

Accommodation (near and far vision).   Accommodation is primarily a function of the lens and undergoes some age-related change that has implications for efficiency of behavior.

The lens becomes more rigid and less pliable with age, the ciliary muscles that help to hold the lens in place may become weaker and lose tone (as do other body muscles), and fast accommodation from near to far (or vice versa) decreases. The far-sightedness associated with age is termed *presbyopia*. Accidents may occur, as for example, missing a step on the stairs, because of lessened ability to shift vision quickly from distant objects to the closer stairs.

Cataracts.   Cataracts are common in older age and are the leading cause of blindness in the United States. There is some debate as to whether cataracts are pathological or a normal age-related change, but since many older persons develop cataracts, they are included here. A cataract consists of increasing cloudiness of the lens. The cause is not completely clear, but many link cataracts to metabolic changes in the proteins of the eye. As cataracts progress, the lens becomes completely opaque and blindness results. Fortunately, cataract surgery is highly successful and age seems to be no significant deterrent to surgery. After cataract removal, compensation for the loss of the original lens is accomplished by lens implantation, contact lenses, or special eyeglasses. Peripheral vision may become restricted and glare more bothersome, however.

Decrease in Adaptation to Dark and Light. Most available data suggest that there is a decrease in light and dark adaptation as one ages. Dark adaptation is the process by which eyes become maximally sensitive to the dark after having been in the light, and light adaptation is the converse. A good example is the experience of walking out of bright sunlight into a dark movie theatre. Initially it is impossible to see anything. After a few minutes the eyes become sensitive to the dark (dark adapted), empty seats can be identified, and individuals can even be recognized. Dark adaptation is a chemical and neural process that takes time for completion. Reasonable sensitivity is usually attained in two to four minutes, although the full chemical process is not complete for about twenty minutes. Conversely, when coming out of a dark theatre into the light, the brightness hurts the eyes for a few minutes until they become light-adapted. Dark and light adaptation are both mediated by chemicals contained in the rods and cones that are bleached out and restored according to prevailing levels of illumination.

Implications of Age-Related Visual Changes

Behavioral implications of changes in vision are primarily associated with accident prevention and the need for eliminating situations in which it is necessary to shift quickly from light to dark areas or vice versa. For instance, driving at night and having to cope with glaring headlights may be hazardous for most older persons due to their slower dark and light adaptation and lessened visual acuity.

The visual system is without question one of the most important links to the world in which we live. A variety of gradual changes take place with age in this very complex system and awareness of these changes should produce greater motivation for preventive care. Attention to regular eye examinations, proper lighting and avoidance of excessive eye strain are important. In addition, there are many effective ways to compensate for visual changes and thereby reduce behavioral limitations related to the aging process. This should be a significant area of interest both to the gerontologist and to older persons as it has enormous practical applications for maintenance of the activities of daily living.

Age-Related Disorders of Vision

"Specks" before the eyes is one age-related condition that tends to increase as one gets older. At times, loose cells and tissue floating in the vitreous humor cast shadows on the retina, causing the specks, but the condition is not in itself a disorder of vision.

Cataracts (see page 59)

Glaucoma

The second leading cause of blindness in the aged (after cataracts) is glaucoma, a major disease of the retina. It is called the "sneak thief" of vision because it progresses slowly and often without warning. Some individuals experience such symptoms as headaches, nausea, vomiting, and seeing halos around lights, but these are often misinterpreted as sinus headaches or other illnesses. Glaucoma is due to the increased production of ocular fluid or to the blockage of the drainage canal for ocular fluid. If excessive fluid accumulates and the intraocular pressure becomes too high, damage to the retina and optic nerve occurs with resultant blindness. Persons over 30 should have periodic glaucoma testing as this disease can usually be controlled if diagnosed early.

Macular Degeneration

Macular degeneration is another major cause of visual impairment in older people. The macula, a spot in the retina which contains the fovea, is the retinal area most densely populated by cones and is responsible for distinct or fine vision. Decreased blood supply to the macula damages receptors and central vision is lost, although peripheral vision may not be affected. Low vision aids such as magnifiers help to offset disabilities due to macular degeneration.

Disorders of the Eyelids

Changes with age may be observed when the eyelids droop and the lids turn inward or outward. Such a condition may cause a corneal ulcer. Many eyelid disorders can be treated by surgery.

HEARING (AUDITION)

Hearing is crucial for humans since much of the time we relate to each other through verbal communication. Hearing loss is thought by many to be the most devastating handicap of all and may result in withdrawal from interaction with society and meaningful people such as family and friends. Paranoid ideas and behavior, isolation, suspicion, and loss of contact with reality are phenomena often observed in the hard of hearing or deaf.

Basic structures of the auditory system are:

● The outer ear, or *pinna,* which is useful in directing sounds from its relatively fixed position into the ear.

● The *middle ear* has great functional significance since the mechanical transmission of sound takes place here. The eardrum, or *tympanic membrane,* separates the outer ear from the middle ear. The *eustachian tubes* provide an opening into the middle ear from the throat and are important in equalizing pressures between the outside and the inside of the head. (Ears "pop" at high altitudes or when skin diving as pressures become equalized.) When extreme pressure differences exist between the outer and middle ear, pain results and the eardrum may rupture unless pressure is equalized.

Structures of importance in the middle ear are three small bones, the *ossicles,* that transmit sound vibrations from the eardrum through the middle ear to the *oval window,* which is covered by a membrane and separates the middle ear from the inner ear.

● The *inner ear* contains two important structures: a) the *cochlea* or auditory organ in which the specific auditory receptors (hair cells) are located, and b) the *vestibular apparatus* (semicircular canals), the receptors for balance and equilibrium. (For this reason an inner ear infection will frequently affect not only hearing, but also equilibrium.)

The auditory receptors are located on the basilar membrane within the cochlea. High, medium, and low tones relate to

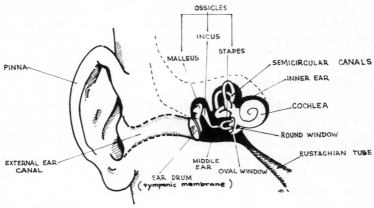

Figure 5. The ear.

different areas of the membrane. Thus it is possible, for example, to have high tone deafness while hearing in the medium and low frequency ranges is relatively intact.

Sound waves enter the outer ear and initiate a vibration of the eardrum, causing the ossicles in the middle ear to move. This movement or vibration passes through the oval window creating a vibration of the fluid in the auditory organ (cochlea) of the inner ear. When the basilar membrane in the cochlea is stimulated, hair cells (the specific auditory receptors) are activated and nerve impulses are sent from the ears via the auditory nerve to the auditory center of the brain. High-frequency sounds vibrate the hair cells on the basal part of the basilar membrane, mid-frequency sounds vibrate those on the middle part of the membrane, and low-frequency sounds primarily vibrate those on the apex of the membrane although they may also involve almost the entire membrane. The auditory nerve contains from 24,000 to 28,000 fibers. The range of human hearing is approximately 20 to 20,000 cycles per second.

The human ear is thus a very sensitive organ, but if it were more sensitive it would be less efficient. For example, a movement of the eardrum of less than one-tenth the diameter of a hydrogen atom can result in an auditory sensation. If the ear were more sensitive it would respond to the movement of air molecules and the resulting roaring sounds would all but mask other auditory stimuli.

Age-Related Changes in Hearing

Subtle changes in hearing usually begin in the 40s and progress gradually with age. It has been estimated that 55 percent of those over age 65 have some hearing loss, while by age 80, 66 percent have serious hearing problems. Specific changes in audition as a result of age include:

Presbycusis

This age-related auditory loss occurs gradually, with the perception of high frequency sounds usually being affected first. Later changes may involve middle and low frequency ranges as well. In our culture, men tend to show hearing loss earlier than women. If the speculation that more males than females have been exposed to high level occupational noise is correct, sex differences in auditory loss could be primarily due to environmental exposure rather than to inherent sex-related differences. Some degree of hearing loss usually occurs in both sexes with time.

Four types of presbycusis can be identified: a) sensory, in which hair cells atrophy, especially at the base of the basilar membrane, causing high-frequency loss; b) neural, in which there is neuron (cell) loss in the auditory nerve itself; c) metabolic, in which tissue in the cochlea dies due to insufficient blood supply; and d) mechanical, in which the ossicles and basilar membrane undergo degenerative changes and become too stiff to function properly.

Changes in Ear Membranes

Age-related changes that occur with age in ear membranes affect one's hearing. The eardrum and the membrane covering the oval window become thickened and more rigid so that sound cannot be transmitted properly.

Changes in Ear Wax

Ear wax (cerumen) thickens and is more difficult to dissolve. Accumulation of ear wax can actually occlude the auditory canal of the outer ear and cause deafness unless removed. Ear wax should be removed by a professional and is not a safe do-it-yourself project.

Implications of Age-Related Changes in Hearing

Since sound can be conducted through the bones of the skull to the inner ear, certain types of deafness are improved by hearing aids while other types of hearing loss cannot be ameliorated by any prosthetic device currently available. Professional evaluation is extremely necessary to accurately assess the possibility of improving hearing with any of the various kinds of aids. Learning to adapt to a hearing aid requires special training and patience since all sound and noise is amplified by most aids. Another concern of those who wear hearing aids is that often others speak too loudly to them, which makes it more rather than less difficult to understand what is being said.

Loss of hearing is usually gradual so that many people compensate well without prosthetic assistance. Instead, they become adept at watching gestures and facial expressions to gain additional information. While many can learn to do this without being formally taught, formal training is extremely helpful to others.

When speaking to someone who has a hearing loss, face the person so you can be seen, speak slowly, enunciate clearly, and lower your voice. Since higher frequency sounds have been found to be the most difficult to discriminate, the suggestion to lower the voice is especially relevant for women, who tend to have higher-pitched voices than most men. Shouting makes voice frequency higher and thus makes speech even more difficult to understand. It is also socially embarrassing to the person who has a hearing loss.

The partially deaf person and the person with normal hearing who is trying to communicate with him/her may both become frustrated with the effort. It is easy to become impatient, give up, and thus deprive the person with impaired hearing of basic social interaction, consigning him/her to a world of silence. We don't continue to communicate if the process becomes too difficult. Also, older persons aren't always willing to admit that their hearing is poor, and their inappropriate responses to words and sentences they've misunderstood may lead to gradual social isolation. Hearing impairment is a potentially devastating phenomenon if those around the older person do not realize the extent of loss and do not consider the behavioral implications for the individual and his/her social world.

People who work with older persons state that there seems to be a degree of selectivity in hearing loss as some individuals hear everything they shouldn't and little that they should. Selectivity is entirely possible, but it is not always voluntary on the elder's part. For example, several specific consonants (g, f, s, z, t, sh, ch) are more difficult than the other sounds to understand and therefore some words are easier to hear than others. Also, a combination of concentration and high motivation enhances ability to compensate for a certain amount of hearing loss.

Age-Related Disorders of Hearing

Otosclerosis

Otosclerosis is due to age-related changes in the bones of the middle ear (ossicles) when they become rigid and unable to function properly. Deafness may result, but surgical intervention is sometimes effective.

Tinnitus

Tinnitus, a condition in which the ears may ring, whistle,

and buzz, is due to changes in the cochlea. Behaviorally it adds to distortion in communication.

Meniere's Syndrome

Meniere's syndrome is primarily observed in middle- and older-aged men. It is due to dysfunction of the labyrinth of the ear. Symptoms include severe dizziness, hearing loss, and buzzing in the ear. Flare-ups and remissions become chronic, but medical or surgical treatment may provide relief.

TASTE (GUSTATION)

Receptors for taste are located primarily in the taste buds on the tongue. Receptors specific to four different taste sensations have been identified. Sweet and salt receptors are predominantly at the tip of the tongue, receptors sensitive to sour are along the sides of the tongue, and those specific to bitter are towards the back of the tongue. Taste is referred to as one of the chemical senses since substances must be in solution to be tasted. Insoluble materials have no taste. Blending of substances produces the variety of taste sensations possible and such variation contributes to the enjoyment of eating.

Age-Related Changes in Taste

Two changes in taste sensitivity have been identified as related to aging. First, the actual number of taste buds declines as some receptors in them atrophy and die. Second, the remaining taste buds evidently have a higher threshold in older people and require a stronger stimulus to activate them. Changes begin in the 40s, but probably do not become too significant for behavior until the 70s or 80s. Although this particular area of research has produced somewhat contradictory evidence, these two changes are generally agreed upon by most authors and are consistent with the types of age-related changes found in the other special sensory systems.

Implications of Age-Related Changes in Taste

Even though basic research has not identified the precise behavioral significance of age changes in taste, it seems possible that the decreased number of receptors over time plus the less efficient functioning of those remaining ought to have some behavioral importance for older persons. Since taste is one of the minor sensory modalities and the changes are gradual, people may not be as aware of changes in taste as of those in vision or hearing.

Many older persons comment about foods tasting bland and regularly pour on salt, sauce, or whatever else is available in an effort to enhance flavor. Eating problems are prevalent among older people confined to institutions. We think it possible that with age foods do begin to taste bland, partially because of changes in the taste receptors themselves. Adding to this complex picture are ill-fitting dentures which often drastically modify eating patterns and the enjoyment of food; eating alone, a situation not conducive to adequately prepared meals; and the loss of appetite from sheer inactivity. A proper diet is important, especially as we grow older, and better education is needed in this area. Nutrition apparently has far-reaching implications for general health and vitality in older age.

SMELL (OLFACTION)

Specific receptors for the sense of smell are located in the nasal passages. Various kinds of receptors have been identified anatomically, but there is no established correlation between types of receptors and the various odors we are capable of differentiating. Data are lacking in this particular sensory system because it is a very difficult research area. We adapt quickly to smell stimuli and are not as dependent upon the sense of smell as are lower animals; thus, olfaction is considered to be a minor sense and of relatively little importance in the human species.

Age-Related Changes in Smell

A decline in the number of fibers in the olfactory nerve has been reported in some research studies, leading to the speculation that smell undergoes age-related changes as do the other sensory systems.

Implication of Age-Related Changes in Smell

If changes do occur in the sense of smell, behavioral implications involve proper ingestion of food, safety, and personal hygiene. For example, the smell of escaping gas fumes from the stove or heater, electrical wires burning, or spoiled foods are highly important cues for personal safety. In addition, smell adds substantially to the pleasure of eating.

SKIN SENSES (CUTANEOUS)

The skin senses are touch, pressure, heat, cold, and pain. Each cutaneous sense has receptors specific to these particular sensations. As with other sensory receptors, differential distribution of cutaneous receptors is found throughout the body. For instance, the fingertips are more sensitive to touch and pressure than is the forearm. According to Steen and Montagu, there are approximately 500,000 points in the skin sensitive to deep pressure, 15,000 sensitive to cold, 16,000 sensitive to heat, and 3 to 4 million sensitive to pain (18).

Age-Related Changes in Skin Senses

Research on age-related changes in the skin senses is sparse. There is some evidence that changes do take place gradually and that such changes are consistent with those in other sensory systems; i.e., loss of receptors with age and increased threshold of stimulation in those remaining.

Implications of Age-Related Changes in Skin Sense

Behavioral implications concern primarily personal safety. Burns are likely to occur if the older person does not accurately perceive temperatures. If touch receptors on the soles of the feet are not functioning effectively, falls occur before the individual even realizes that the foot is not on a solid surface. Touch is necessary in order to orient ourselves to many aspects of the daily environment and to prevent accidents.

Evidence pertaining to changes in perception of temperature and pain is less clear. Clinical observations suggest that, with age, there is greater susceptibility to extremes of heat and cold and decreased sensitivity to pain. If true, these factors should be taken into account in working with older individuals and in planning practical life environments for older age groups.

VESTIBULAR AND KINESTHETIC SENSES

Receptors for the vestibular (balance and equilibrium) sense are located in the semicircular canals of the inner ear. These receptors are responsive to changes of body position in space, and they function in the maintenance of equilibrium and the coordination of movements of the body.

Receptors for the *kinesthetic* sense, located in muscles and tendons, provide information on joint movement as well as body position in space. The kinesthetic system is often called the "muscle sense."

Age-Related Changes in Vestibular and Kinesthetic Senses

There is some evidence from basic research and clinical observation that age-related changes in both the vestibular and the kinesthetic sensory systems lead to higher thresholds of stimulation and therefore to decreased behavioral efficiency. Body sway increases with age and may be partially responsible for general postural unsteadiness (especially falls) experienced by many older persons. Equilibrium and balance become impaired, especially when fast movement is required. Older persons generally adapt by moving slowly and walking with a wide-stance-feet-apart gait to provide greater stability. The pacing of movements is much more important in older age, not only for conserving energy but also for safety.

THE IMPORTANCE OF SENSORY CHANGES IN THE AGING

Sensory changes with age are some of the most crucial and possibly the most underrated changes associated with the entire aging process. Perhaps it is because these changes usually occur gradually and are not as dramatic as other handicaps that occur suddenly through accident or health crises. Perhaps our lack of active concern in this area arises from the "error of familiarity," as most people are at least vaguely aware that sensory changes take place with age but do not dwell on the possible implications of such changes. Perhaps we tend to write these changes off with a "what can you expect from old age?" attitude. Whatever the reasons, most people who are interested and involved in the study of the aging process do not give sensory changes and their cumulating impact the significance they deserve.

Changes in each of these systems interfere with the ability to gather pertinent information about the environment essential to high-quality life, and even to the maintenance of life itself. Is it not reasonable, then, that as sensory changes gradually occur, the organism experiences sensory deprivation that may lead to social isolation as individuals become less mobile, more housebound, or more difficult to engage in communication? Next might well be "functional senility," a state in which the person generates his/her own world of fantasy since the real world is not interesting enough to provide the variety of stimulation needed to keep psychologically intact.

BIBLIOGRAPHY

Books

Agate, John. *The Practice of Geriatrics,* 2nd ed. Springfield, Ill.: Charles C Thomas, 1970.

Birren, James E. *The Psychology of Aging.* Englewood Cliffs, N. J.: Prentice-Hall, 1964.

Botwinick, Jack. *Aging and Behavior.* New York: Springer Publishing Co., 1973.

Burnside, Irene M. The special senses and sensory deprivation. In Burnside, Irene M., ed., *Nursing and the Aged.* New York: McGraw-Hill, 1976.

Engen, Trygg. Taste and smell. In Birren, James E. and Schaie, K. Warner, eds., *Handbook of the Psychology of Aging.* New York: Van Nostrand Reinhold, 1977.

Ernst, Marin and Shore, Herbert. *Sensitizing People to the Processes of Aging: The In-service Educator's Guide.* Denton, Texas: Center for Studies in Aging, North Texas State University, 1975.

Hickey, Tom and Fatula, Betty. *Sensory Deprivation and the Elderly (Training Module).* University Park, Pa.: The Gerontology Center, The Pennsylvania State University, 1975.

Hodkinson, H. M. *An Outline of Geriatrics.* New York: Academic Press, 1975.

Kammerman, Mark, ed., *Sensory Isolation and Personality Change.* Springfield, Ill.: Charles C Thomas, 1977.

Pfaltz, C. R. Diseases of the ear and of the vestibular system. In von Hahn, H. P., ed., *Practical Geriatrics.* Basel: Karger, 1975.

Rintelen, F. Diseases of the eye. In von Hahn, H. P., ed., *Practical Geriatrics.* Basel: Karger, 1975.

Seligman, Martin E. P. *Helplessness.* San Francisco: Freeman, 1975.

Solomon, P., Kubzansky, P. E. and Leiderman, P. H. *et al.,* eds., *Sensory Deprivation.* Cambridge: Harvard Press, 1961.

Thompson, Richard F. *Introduction to Physiological Psychology.* New York: Harper and Row, 1975.

Periodicals

Bergman, Moe. Changes in hearing with age. *Gerontologist 11:*148, 1971.

Beverly, E. V. Reducing fire and burn hazards among the elderly. *Geriatrics 31:*106, 1976.

Black, F. O. Vestibular causes of vertigo. *Geriatrics 30:*123, 1975.

Burnside, Irene M. Touching is talking. *American Journal of Nursing 73:*2060, 1973.

Buseck, S. A. Visual status of the elderly. *Journal of Gerontological Nursing 2:*34, 1976.

Cooper, A. F. and Curry, A. R. The pathology of deafness in the paranoid and affective psychoses of later life. *Journal of Psychosomatic Research 20:*97, 1976.

Cooper, A. F. and Porter, R. Visual acuity and ocular pathology in the paranoid and affective psychoses of later life. *Journal of Psychosomatic Research 20:*104, 1976.

Corso, John. Sensory processes and age effects in normal adults. *Journal of Gerontology 26:*90, 1971.

Fonda, G. E. Ways to improve vision in partially sighted persons. *Geriatrics 30:*49, 1975.

Gaitz, C. and Warshaw, H. Obstacles encountered in correcting hearing loss in the elderly. *Geriatrics 19:*83, 1964.

Harrison, R. Glaucoma in the elderly. *Geriatrics 30:*55, 1975.

Hill, D. W. The management of visual loss. *Proceedings of the Royal Society of Medicine 66:164, 1973.*

Kornzweig, Abraham. The prevention of blindness in the aged. *Journal of the American Geriatrics Society 20:*383, 1972.

McArdle, C. Communicating with hard of hearing patients. *Age and Ageing 4:*116, 1975.

Mathog, R. H., Paprella, M. M., Huff, J., Seigel, L., Lassman, F. and Bozarth, M. Common hearing disorders. Methods of diagnosis and treatment. *Geriatrics 29:*49, 1974.

Meyerson, Marion. The effects of aging upon communication. *Journal of Gerontology 31:*29, 1976.

O'Neil, P. M. and Calhoun, K. S. Sensory deficits and behavioral deterioration in senescence. *Journal of Abnormal Psychology 84:*579, 1975.

Oster, C. Sensory deprivation in geriatric patients. *Journal of the American Geriatrics Society 24:*461, 1976.

Phythyon, Marlin and McConnell, Freeman. Hearing rehabilitation for older people. *Gerontologist 9:*66, 1969.

Richards, S. Deafness in the elderly. *Gerontologica Clinica 13:*350, 1971.

Ronis, M. L., Liebman, E. P. and Lindsay, C. H. The rehabilitation of the aged deaf. *Geriatrics 26:*57, 1971.

Rupp, R. R. Understanding the problems of presbycusis. An overview of hearing loss associated with aging. *Geriatrics 25:*100, 1970.

Shore, Herbert. Designing a training program for understanding sensory losses in aging. *Gerontologist 16:*157, 1976.

Slaughter, T. Vision care for the elderly. *Modern Health Care 4:*47, 1975.

Sloane, A. E. and Kraut, J. A. The pleasures of reading need not diminish with age. *Geriatrics 30:*117, 1975.

Snyder, L. H., Pyrek, J. and Smith, K. C. Vision and mental function of the elderly. *Gerontologist 16:*491, 1976.

Van der Laan, F. L. and Oosterveld, W. J. Age and vestibular function. *Aerospace Medicine 45:*540, 1974.

Van Heyningen, R. What happens to the human lens in cataract. *Scientific American 233:*70, 1975.

Weiss, Curtis. Why more of the aged with auditory deficits do not wear hearing aids. *Journal of the American Geriatrics Society 21:*139, 1973.

Unit 7

The Circulatory System

The circulatory system moves certain body fluids through two subsystems: the blood-vascular system *and the* lymphatic system. *Both blood and lymph systems are important transportation mechanisms in the human body and each has a vital role to play.*

FUNCTIONS OF BLOOD

Blood, the major medium for the transportation of fluids throughout the body, has a number of significant functions in the maintenance of life and health. These functions are:

1. *Respiratory,* through the distribution of oxygen from the lungs to the tissues of the body for cell use, and of carbon dioxide from the body tissues back to the lungs where it is expelled.

2. *Nutritive,* through the transport of food substances such as glucose, fats, and amino acids from storage places (intestines, for example) to body tissues where these materials are needed to produce energy and to maintain life.

3. *Excretory,* through the movement of waste products from body cells to the excretory organs.

4. *Protective,* through movement of antibodies in the body to assist in resisting disease and infection.

5. *Regulatory,* through the control of body equilibrium (homeostasis) in general, and specifically through hormone distribution, maintenance of water balance, and temperature regulation. For example, excess heat generated in the body is transported continuously to the lungs and to the body surface where it is dissipated.

THE BLOOD-VASCULAR SYSTEM

The human blood-vascular organizational plan is a closed system in which damage to any part will ultimately affect the entire system. The major components of the blood-vascular system are:

● The *heart*, a pumping organ.

● The *arteries,* which are tubes that conduct blood from the heart to the body cells. The smallest of the artery branches are called *arterioles.*

● The *veins*, which are tubes that conduct blood from body tissues back to the heart. The smallest of the vein branches are called *venules.*

● The *capillaries,* minute blood vessels connecting the arterioles with the venules.

Various estimates suggest that the body contains about 70,000 miles of blood vessels, the majority being capillaries.

The Heart

The pump of the system is the heart, a hollow organ with highly muscular walls, which is situated between the lungs and slightly to the left of the midline of the chest (the thoracic cavity). In complex organisms such as humans, the heart has four chambers: two atria (upper chambers) and two ventricles (lower chambers). A thick partition separates the left side of the heart from the right. The largest artery of the body (the aorta) leads out of the left ventricle, and the pulmonary artery emerges from the right ventricle. The largest veins of the body (superior and inferior vena cavae) enter the right atrium while the pulmonary veins enter the left atrium. The atria and the ventricles are separated by valves that control both the location and the amount of blood in each of the four chambers of the heart. The left valve is called the *mitral* or *bicuspid* and the right valve the *tricuspid. Semilunar valves* separate each ventricle and its specific artery (aorta or pulmonary); no valves are found between the atria and their respective veins (venae cavae or pulmonary).

Since the heart is composed of muscle tissue it must have a rich blood supply in order to maintain proper functioning. This circulation involves specific coronary arteries branching from the base of the aorta and distributing blood to the walls of the heart. Veins collect the blood to be returned to the right atrium

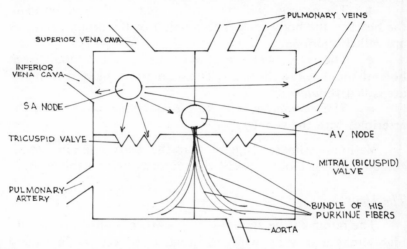

Figure 6A. Schema of the electrical conduction system of the heart.

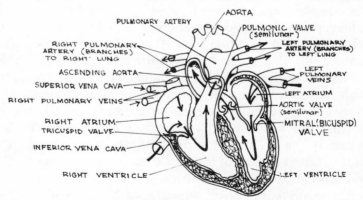

Figure 6B. The heart, showing vessels, chambers, and direction of blood flow.

through a large vein called the *coronary sinus*. If any of the coronary arteries become occluded and block the supply of oxygen and other nutrients to heart muscle, a heart attack results.

Blood Circulation

There are two blood circuits, one called *systemic,* supplying all body parts, and the other called *pulmonary,* circulating blood through the lungs for blood purification.

● Systemic circulation depends upon the movement of purified, oxygen rich blood from the left ventricle of the heart through the largest artery of the body (the aorta) and its various tree-like branches to all body tissues and cells. The smallest arterial capillaries connect to venules which, in turn, are connected to larger and larger veins, and ultimately to the two largest veins in the body, the superior and inferior venae cavae, which empty into the right atrium of the heart.

● Pulmonary circulation involves blood flow from the right ventricle into the pulmonary artery and thence to the lungs. There carbon dioxide is removed from the blood, which then takes on a new supply of fresh oxygen. Pulmonary veins transport the oxygen-rich blood back to the left atrium of the heart, from which it passes into the left ventricle. After leaving the left ventricle, it again courses through the body in the systemic circulation circuit. Consequently, the right side of the heart receives oxygen-poor blood from body tissues, while the left side of the heart receives oxygen-rich blood from the lungs.

Blood circulates through the body as follows: oxygen-rich blood from the lungs enters the left atrium via the pulmonary veins; when the atrium fills with blood it contracts, the mitral valve opens and blood flows into the left ventricle. Since the valve is a one-way device, blood flows only from the atrium to the ventricle. When the left ventricle fills with blood it contracts, the semilunar valve opens, and blood is then forced into the aorta, after which the valve closes so that blood cannot reenter the ventricle. Blood circulates throughout the body by way of the aorta and its branches, connects with veins at the level of the capillaries, and returns to the right atrium of the heart via the network of veins. When the right atrium fills, the tricuspid valve opens and deoxygenated blood passes into the right ventricle. After blood fills the right ventricle, the ventricle contracts and forces blood past the semilunar valve into the pulmonary artery to be carried to the lungs and oxygenated. Oxygenated blood returns to the left atrium via the pulmonary veins and the cycle begins again. The heart beats at a rate of about 72 times a minute, or about 100,000 times a day. More than 4,000 gallons of blood is pumped through the heart every day.

Contractions of the atria and ventricles, the opening and closing of the heart valves, and the shunting of blood through the chambers of the heart generate the various heart sounds useful to physicians in assessing functional status of the heart.

Blood Pressure

The contraction of the left ventricle forces blood into the aorta with a definite force or pressure. The pressure resulting from ventricular contraction is called *systolic* and represents the upper number of a blood pressure reading. During the subsequent relaxation of the ventricle, pressure decreases and this represents the *diastolic* pressure, the lower number of a blood pressure reading. According to most authorities, average blood pressure should be about 120/80 although it must be emphasized that blood pressure fluctuates according to the individual's physiological and psychological status of the moment. Even though 120/80 represents the average, a variation in readings around this figure may be considered normal. Several blood pressure readings need to be taken at different times before hypertension or hypotension (too high or too low blood pressure) can be diagnosed.

Some of the many factors influencing blood pressure are a) age (blood pressure tends to increase with age); b) pumping action of the heart (varies with age and health); c) blood volume (the amount of blood pumped); d) elasticity of arterial walls (determines how easy or how difficult it is for blood to flow); e) thickness or thinness of blood (affects rate of blood flow); f) peripheral resistance (especially in the limbs).

Maintenance of Circulation

Circulation is maintained through the continuous rhythmic action of the heart. Although the nervous system affects heart rate, heart muscle is unlike other muscles of the body in that it is self-excitatory and has its own built-in pacemaker mechanism to maintain its rhythmic and coordinated activity. Specifically, the heart beat is initiated by a segment of tissue in the right atrium designated as the sinoatrial (S-A) node. Excitation begun at the S-A node spreads to similar nodal tissue, the atrioventricular (A-V) node at the junction of the right atrium and right ventricle, and then through a bundle of fibers (bundle of His) to the ventricle walls. Normally the atria and ventricles beat in a coordinated rhythm at approximately 72 times a minute. If injury or disease interferes with impulse transmission between S-A and A-V nodes, though, atria and ventricles beat at different rates and heart block results. In certain instances heart rhythm is disrupted and random contractions (fibrillation) occur.

LYMPHATIC SYSTEM

The lymphatic system is composed of:

● *Lymph,* a tissue fluid.

● *Lymph capillaries,* very small vessels within body tissues.

● A system of *lymph vessels* which transport lymph from tissues to the *lymph ducts* and carry lymph to the bloodstream.

The major functions of the lymphatic system are:

1. To return to the bloodstream tissue fluid that has filtered out of blood capillaries.

2. To assist in the prevention of the spread of infection and disease by straining out foreign particles and bacteria as the lymph passes through special lymphoid tissue (such as tonsils, adenoids, and lymph nodes).

Age-Related Changes in the Circulatory System

While some cells such as skin or blood cells are self-replenishing, cardiac cells are not replaced once damaged or destroyed. The original cells must last for a lifetime.

Structural Changes

Normally, heart size does not change significantly with age. According to Agate (19), it is not unusual to find the heart of an older person anatomically, clinically, and electrically indistinguishable from the heart of a young person. Contrary to some popular opinions, an enlarged heart is not normal in old age and may instead suggest possible pathology. Changes that do commonly occur include:

1. The amount of fatty tissue in the heart increases.
2. The heart valves become more rigid and thicker.
3. Thickening, hardening, and lessening of elasticity of walls of blood vessels occurs, especially in arteries.

Arteriosclerosis and *atherosclerosis* are two vascular problems associated with growing older.

Arteriosclerosis. This is a general term for vascular changes leading to progressive thickening and loss of resiliency (inelasticity) of arterial walls (also referred to as hardening of the arteries).

Atherosclerosis. This is a form of arteriosclerosis in which fatty-type deposits appear within the arteries and gradually occlude the channel of the artery. A descriptive analogy is that of rust accumulating on the inner surface of a metal water pipe and gradually constricting the opening until eventually water can no longer flow through. Even if actual occlusion does not occur, atherosclerosis creates rough surfaces on inner arterial walls that become ideal sites for blood clots to form. Atherosclerosis principally affects the large and medium sized arteries—the aorta (arising from the heart and supplying blood to the entire body); the coronary arteries (supplying blood to heart muscle itself); and the arteries supplying blood to the brain, abdomen, and legs.

Both arteriosclerosis and atherosclerosis lead to increases in blood pressure, produce extra stress on the heart muscle, and set the stage for other diseases in the cardiovascular system. The heart must work harder but with less overall effect, resulting in less oxygen delivered to body cells and decreased efficiency of body organs in performing their necessary activities. Age-related circulatory inefficiency is always more evident in stress situations than in normal activities of daily living.

Functional Changes

Longer Recovery.   Older heart muscle requires a longer time to recover after each beat, or in other words, the heart requires a slightly longer rest period between beats. This fact is not significant in normal activity, but it may limit behavior in situations in which the heart is stressed and required to beat faster than normal. Consequently, older people may be more prone to heart failure than the young, who have greater reserve capacity in heart functioning.

Arrhythmias.   At rest, heart rate in people of older age is essentially the same as in younger people; however, some authors suggest that arrhythmias such as skipped or extra beats become more common with age. Arrhythmias sometimes produce anxiety in older persons who fail to understand that this is not necessarily indicative of heart disease. On the other hand, the aging heart is less able to increase its rate in response to stress.

Decline in Cardiac Output.   Cardiac output (the amount of blood pumped from the heart in one minute) declines with age, causing less oxygen to be delivered to body tissues and organs. An 80-year-old individual receives one-third less oxygen into his/her system than does a 20-year-old, and by age 90 blood volume pumped by the heart is estimated to have decreased approximately 50 percent from what it was at age 20.

Reduced cardiac output occurs both at rest and with exercise, but the decline is often of minimal consequence for normal everyday behavior. Nevertheless, this fact may help to explain why most older people tire more quickly than the young and why endurance, especially in strenuous work, tends to decline with age. In summary, in nonstressful conditions the normal aging heart functions adequately, although more slowly than formerly, but under stress the effects of age become increasingly obvious and gradually lead to limitations in behavior. Current research suggests that one way to promote continued adequate cardiac output is through regular, systematic exercise. Walking is one of the best and safest ways for older persons to exercise and involves no expensive equipment or special place.

Changes in Arteries and Veins.   In our society the aging process seems to affect the arteries more than the heart itself as the arteries and, to a lesser extent, the veins become less elastic and less flexible. Elasticity of arteries is a major factor in regulating blood pressure. For instance, in excitement the heart beats faster and more blood is pumped through the body at an increased rate. The elastic arterial walls normally expand to accommodate the greater force of blood pushed through and thus arterial resistance is decreased. If the arterial walls are rigid and cannot expand, the heart must pump harder to move more blood through the system quickly. Blood pressure increases as arterial resistance is increased. Such increases in blood pressure are a common corollary of the aging process.

Age-Related Disorders of the Circulatory System

Hypertension

Persistent abnormally high blood pressure is prevalent in many of the elderly (and middle-agers) and is associated not only with arteriosclerosis but also with other factors or systems involved in regulating blood pressure. Four body systems are particularly involved in hypertension: 1) the cardiovascular system, because of its tendency toward sclerosis (hardening of the arteries; 2) the endocrine system, when it acts to retain sodium chloride or salt in the body; 3) the excretory system, when excess amounts of renin are secreted, or when the kidneys do not excrete sodium, and water is drawn back from the urinary tubules into the blood; and 4) the nervous system, because it responds to excessive and prolonged emotional tension by producing an increase in peripheral resistance to blood flow, often reflected as high blood pressure.

Unfortunately, many individuals have hypertension and never experience symptoms until organ functions become impaired. Even if there are signs of headache, dizziness, or fatigue, these may or may not be associated with hypertension. The only way to be certain is to have blood pressure checked periodically. Long-term, untreated hypertension may cause: enlargement of the heart, possibly with eventual heart failure; further and more widespread arteriosclerosis; possible rupture of blood vessels, especially in the brain (stroke); and kidney dysfunction.

Coronary Heart Disease

The blood that passes through the heart doesn't nourish the heart itself. It is the coronary arteries, branching from the aorta, that supply blood directly to the heart muscle. Coronary heart disease results when the blood supply through these arteries is reduced or blocked in any of the following ways:

1. Too high blood pressure in the coronary arteries may result in *hemorrhage* if a blood vessel should rupture.

2. An *aneurysm,* which is a weak spot in a coronary arterial wall, may rupture, causing a hemorrhage.

3. If *blood clots* form, they may restrict or block blood flow through the coronary arteries.

4. *Fatty deposits* (atherosclerosis) in inner walls of coronary arteries sometimes interfere with blood flow to heart muscle. This is the most frequent cause of heart disease in older persons.

If, because of reduced blood flow, insufficient oxygen reaches the heart via the coronary arteries, heart rhythm becomes erratic or may cease altogether. Coronary heart disease manifests itself either suddenly in a "heart attack," or more gradually, as angina pectoris.

No attempt will be made to elaborate the variety of conditions subsumed under the lay term "heart attack;" rather, only two of the more common heart problems are considered here: myocardial infarction and heart failure.

Myocardial Infarction. Myocardial infarction is an occlusion of either an artery or vein resulting in complete interference with blood supply to a part of the heart muscle. Severe pain may or may not accompany myocardial infarction. Symptoms may be similar to those of indigestion or general abdominal discomfort.

Heart failure. Prolonged, inadequate oxygen supply to the heart is a major cause of heart failure, although conditions such as acute bronchitis, emphysema, alcoholism, pneumonia, kidney disease, and obesity are also causative factors. Typical warning signs of impending heart attack are a squeezing pain in the center of the chest, pain radiating to shoulder, arm, or neck, sweating, nausea, and shortness of breath. In elderly persons the pain may not be as intense as in younger persons or reported as accurately, and since the symptoms associated with digestion, gallbladder, and respiratory ailments may also be similar to those of a heart attack, utmost caution is necessary in interpreting all complaints of pain and discomfort.

Angina Pectoris.   The term angina pectoris is Latin for "chest pain." It occurs when the heart muscle is not receiving an adequate blood supply for effective functioning. Attacks are characterized by severe pain radiating from the chest area to the left shoulder and down the left arm accompanied by feelings of pressure, tightness, or suffocation. Anginal attacks are often precipitated by excitement, muscular activity, a large meal, or very cold weather, but they may also occur when the person is at rest. Medication is usually effective and environmental manipulation to avoid stress and excitement is also important. Sometimes collateral circulation develops as new branches of the coronary artery evolve and are able to provide adequate blood supply to the heart.

Risk factors that significantly increase the chances of heart attack are age, elevated cholesterol, smoking, hypertension, obesity, diabetes, inactivity, and a family history of heart attack. In this country, heart disease is the most common cause of death in persons over 65; strokes are the second most common cause. Together, these two disease entities account for almost ten times the rate of the next common cause of death—cancer.

Stroke (Cerebrovascular Accident)

About 200,000 people in the United States die from strokes annually. Three-fourths of these deaths occur in persons over 70 years of age. A stroke is referred to as a cerebrovascular accident (CVA) and is a condition in which the blood supply to the brain is reduced or completely shut off. The most common cause of stroke in older persons is a cerebral thrombosis or blood clot that either diminishes or closes off the blood flow in an artery of the brain or neck. Brain cells supplied by this artery may then die from lack of vital oxygen. The cells of the nervous system are extremely sensitive to a lack of adequate oxygen. Other possible causes of a stroke are cerebral hemorrhage, which occurs when a weak spot in a blood vessel of the brain bursts, and atherosclerosis, in which fatty deposits gradually occlude an artery in the brain or neck.

Strokes affect behavior in many different ways depending upon the functions of the part of the brain that is damaged by the stroke. Muscle movements, speech, memory, or emotions may be impaired. Some strokes are severe, others mild, and this is why certain people recover extremely well, others partially or never.

"Small strokes" (transient ischemic episodes) are early indications of impairment in blood supply to the brain. Behavioral changes following small strokes may be so minimal that only close family members realize that some subtle change, often in personality or mood, has taken place. Unfortunately, these early warning signs are frequently ignored or attributed to other causes and the potentiality for a major stroke increases. According to the American Heart Association (20) signs of a "little stroke" may include:

● Sudden, temporary weakness or numbness of face, arm, or leg.
● Temporary difficulty in speech, loss of speech, or trouble understanding speech.
● Brief dimness or loss of vision, particularly in one eye.
● Double vision.
● Unexplained headaches or a change in the kind of headaches.
● Temporary dizziness or unsteadiness.
● Recent change in personality or mental ability.

Rehabilitation following a stroke is often successful if started early. In addition to the physical symptoms manifested, however, family and friends must be especially sensitive to strong emotional reactions such as depression, confusion, emotional instability, inappropriate emotional responses, and fear following stroke. To be maximally effective, rehabilitation must meet not only the physical needs, but also psychological and social needs of the individual and his/her family.

Aneurysm

Aneurysm is a term used to describe a "pouch" formed in a weakened arterial wall. The pouch fills with blood and, if the arterial wall is too weak and the blood pressure too great, it may burst. Such a problem is especially serious when the aneurysm is large and involves the abdominal aorta or cerebral blood vessels.

Phlebitis

Phlebitis is an inflammation of a vein, often in the leg. Phlebitis produces conditions favorable for the formation of blood clots that may break loose and occlude a major vessel or move into the lungs with very serious consequences.

Varicose Veins

Varicose veins are swollen, "knotted" veins, usually in the lower extremities and caused by a weakening of venous walls. They are more prevalent in females and the obese, and a predisposition to varicosities occurs in families. Varicose veins in the lower part of the rectum and anus are called *hemorrhoids*.

Implications of Age-Related Circulatory System Disorders

It is imperative to recognize that circulatory problems and disease frequently lead to fear and anxiety, increasing preoccupation with self, possible impatience with those who are healthy, and a tendency to restrict life style or modify it from activity to inactivity. These are not therapeutically desirable behaviors and efforts should be directed to reinstating as normal a life style as possible after a dramatic health episode involving circulatory system impairment or disease. Many people with circulatory disease live very normal, well-balanced lives under medical supervision and take better care of themselves (without undue overconcern or preoccupation with self) than many of us who do not have such medical problems.

BIBLIOGRAPHY

Books

American Medical Association. *The Wonderful Human Machine*. Chicago: American Medical Association, 1971.

Caird, F. I. and Dall, J. L. C. The Cardiovascular system. In Brocklehurst, J. C., ed. *Textbook of Geriatric Medicine and Gerontology*. Edinburgh and London: Churchill and Livingstone, 1973.

Chinn, Austin B., ed. *Working with Older People: Vol. IV Clinical Aspects of Aging*. Rockville, Md.: U. S. Department of Health, Education, and Welfare, 1971.

Hardin, William B. Neurological aspects. In Steinburg, Franz, ed., *Cowdry's the Care of the Geriatric Patient,* 5th ed. St. Louis: Mosby, 1976.

Harris, Raymond. Cardiac problems: treating the geriatric patient. In Busse, Ewald, ed., *Theory and Therapeutics of Aging*. New York: Medcom, 1973.

Kohn, Robert R. Heart and cardiovascular system. In Finch, Caleb E. and Hayflick, Leonard, eds., *Handbook of the Biology of Aging*. New York: Van Nostrand Reinhold, 1977.

Lorenze, Edward J. Stroke. In Busse, Ewald, ed., *Theory and Therapeutics of Aging*. New York: Medcom, 1973.

Milne, L. J. and Milne, M. *The Ages of Life*. New York: Harcourt, 1968.

Steen, Edwin B. and Montagu, Ashley. *Anatomy and Physiology* Vol. 1. New York: Barnes and Noble, 1959.

Timiras, P. S. Cardiovascular alterations with age: atherosclerosis. In Timiras, P. S., ed., *Developmental Physiology and Aging.* New York: Macmillan, 1972.

Periodicals

Alvarez, Walter. A reminder about little strokes. *Geriatrics 20:*159, 1974.

Benditt, E. P. The origin of atherosclerosis. *Scientific American 236:*74, 1977.

Blumenthal, H. T. and Alex, M. Special issue on athero-arteriosclerosis. An iconoclastic view of current concepts concerning genesis, prevention and control. *Gerontologica Clinica 21:*131, 1975.

Burch, G. E. The special problems of heart disease in old people. *Geriatrics 32:*51, 1977.

Chobanian, A. V. Hypertension: major risk factor for cardiovascular complications. *Geriatrics 31:*87, 1976.

Chrysant, S. G., Frohlich, E. D. and Papper, S. Why hypertension is so prevalent in the elderly—and how to treat it. *Geriatrics 31:*101, 1976.

Edwards, A. E. and Hart, G. M. Hyperbaric oxygenation and the cognitive functioning of the aged. *Journal of the American Geriatrics Society 22:*376, 1974.

Feldman, J. L. and Schultz, M. E. Rehabilitation after stroke. *Cardiovascular Nursing 11:*29, 1975.

Harris, Raymond. The management of geriatric cardiovascular disease. *Gerontologist 11:*253, 1971.

Isaacs, B., Neville, Y. and Rushford, I. The stricken: the social consequences of stroke. *Age and Ageing 5:*188, 1976.

Librach, G., Schadel, M., Seltzer, M., Hart, A. and Yellin, N. Stroke: incidence and risk factors. *Geriatrics 32:*85, 1977.

Martin, A. and Millard, P. H. Cardiovascular assessment in the elderly. *Age and Ageing 2:*211, 1973.

Pomerance, A. The many facets of cardiac pathology. *Geriatrics 28:*110, 1973.

Robbins, S. Stroke in the geriatric patient. *Hospital Practitioner 11:*33, 1976.

Syzek, B. J. Cardiovascular changes in aging: implications for nursing. *Journal of Gerontological Nursing 2:*28, 1976.

Vavrik, M. "High risk" factors and atherosclerotic cardiovascular diseases in the aged. *Journal of the American Geriatric Society 22:*203, 1974.

Wedgwood, J. Heart failure in old age. *Postgraduate Medicine 52:*179, 1972.

Unit 8

The Respiratory System

The structures comprising the respiratory system are:

- The various air passageways, including nasal cavities, mouth, pharynx, larynx, trachea, bronchi, bronchioles, alveolar ducts, and alveoli.
- The lungs.

AIR PASSAGEWAYS

Air enters the body primarily through the *nasal cavities,* where it is warmed, moistened, and filtered by the mucous membranes in the nose, but it may also enter through the mouth. Either way, incoming air enters the *pharynx,* the tube leading into both the larynx (the route to the lungs) and the esophagus (the route to the stomach). Seven cavities or tubes open into the pharynx: mouth, trachea, esophagus, two nostrils and two eustachian tubes. The tonsils are located in the pharyngeal area and serve to protect these orifices against bacterial infection.

Passing through the pharynx, air enters the *larynx* (or voice box since it contains the vocal cords), a structure composed of nine cartilages bound together by an elastic-like membrane. One of the cartilages, the thyroid cartilage, is ordinarily more prominent in men than in women and is referred to as the "Adam's apple." Following puberty the larynx becomes larger in males and the vocal cords become longer and thicker; as a result, men tend to have deeper voices than women. Human voice quality, with all of its variations and complexities, involves not only the larynx, but the pharynx, nasal cavities, mouth, teeth, tongue, resonating chambers in the head (sinuses), and the learned ability to control the inhalation and exhalation of air.

Extending from the larynx through the neck and into the chest area (the thorax) is the *trachea,* or "windpipe." The trachea, situated in front of the esophagus, is composed of elastic tissue and from 16 to 20 cartilage rings. The trachea thus has some flexibility and elasticity, but not enough to allow it to collapse and cut off the air supply to the lungs.

Upon entering the chest region the trachea divides into left and right *bronchi* (smaller tubes) that lead into the lungs. The bronchi divide into smaller and smaller tubes until, at about 1 millimeter in diameter, they become tiny elastic tubes called *bronchioles.* Bronchioles branch into even smaller *alveolar ducts* leading to many finger-like projections, the *alveoli* (air sacs). The minute alveoli are in contact with the many blood capillaries in the lungs where diffusion of materials between alveoli and blood takes place. It is here that carbon dioxide, a waste product, is removed from the blood and a fresh supply of oxygen is picked up by the blood to be delivered to body tissues for immediate use. Hemoglobin in the blood cells is necessary for effective carbon dioxide-oxygen exchange. This blood purification process is the main function of the respiratory system.

To summarize, the "bronchial tree" is composed of a series of tubes that become progressively smaller until they end in a network of alveoli in contact with the blood capillaries. The life sustaining carbon dioxide-oxygen exchange occurs here.

THE LUNGS

The *lungs* are the major organs of respiration. The two lungs are soft, spongy, elastic tissue able to change shape during respiratory movements. They are located in the chest, or thoracic cavity, and are somewhat cone-shaped. The top or apex extends into the base of the neck, while the lower part of the lungs rests on the diaphragm, a large muscle forming the partition between the thoracic and abdominal cavities. The left lung is divided into two parts, or lobes, while the right lung has three lobes. Each lung is enclosed in a membrane called the *pleura.*

FUNCTIONS OF THE RESPIRATORY SYSTEM

Breathing

Movements of the respiratory muscles allow for changes in the size of the chest or thoracic cavity and make breathing possible. During inspiration or inhalation, for example, the size of the chest is increased by the contraction and flattening of the diaphragm and by contraction of the rib cage muscles, causing the ribs to move upward and forward. As a result, chest capacity increases, pressure within the lungs decreases, and air is sucked in. As the respiratory muscles relax, the diaphragm resumes its normal dome shape, the ribs move back to resting position,

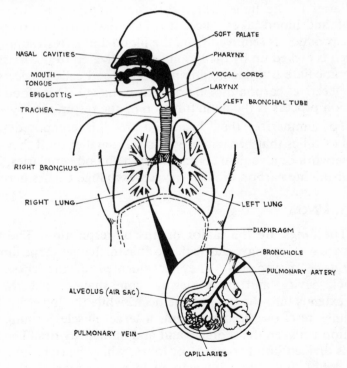

Figure 7. The respiratory system and alveoli.

and chest volume (size) decreases. As the size of the chest cavity becomes smaller, pressure in the lungs increases and air is forced out (expiration or exhalation).

Thus, the action necessary for breathing is not a function of the lungs alone, but is primarily due to the action of diaphragm and rib cage muscles. The lungs are not muscular tissues, but act more like balloons subject to pressure differences between the lung cavity in the body and atmospheric pressures outside the body. They are sometimes compared to a bellows in action.

Respiration rate is essentially under involuntary control by brain centers in the medulla (at the base of the brain), although it is also subject to substantial voluntary control. We cannot voluntarily breathe while swallowing, though, because of a powerful reflex that prevents food or liquids from passing down the trachea to the lungs instead of down the esophagus to the stomach. When this reflex is interfered with in any way, we choke. There is another strong reflex regulating breathing that is controlled essentially by carbon dioxide levels in the blood. When the amount of carbon dioxide exceeds a certain level, we are forced to breathe. Carbon dioxide level in the blood, then, controls breathing more than the level of oxygen.

External and Internal Respiration

The exchange in the lungs of oxygen from the air and carbon dioxide from the blood is called *external respiration*. The exchange in the body cells of oxygen from the blood and carbon dioxide from the tissues constitutes *internal respiration*. Both processes are necessary for the maintenance of life. Body cells are highly dependent upon a constant supply of oxygen for metabolism and upon the regular pick-up and excretion of carbon dioxide, a major waste product of body metabolic processes. Since body cells and tissues are unable to store any significant amount of oxygen over time, a new supply must be delivered continuously to all tissues of the body via the bloodstream. Cells die rapidly without oxygen.

Age-Related Changes in the Respiratory System

Although age-related changes occur in the respiratory system, such changes are quite difficult to determine. The prevalence of environmental factors such as air pollution, occupational hazards, and cigarette smoking obviously complicate the picture of nonpathological aging.

Nevertheless, respiratory efficiency does seem to change with age for the following reasons:

1. Skeletal changes such as calcification of the costal (rib) cartilages, osteoporosis, kyphosis ("humpback"), and scoliosis (lateral spinal curvature, often S-shaped) limit rib cage expansion.

2. The muscles responsible for inhalation and exhalation movements may become weakened and atrophied as a part of the aging process. Since these muscles are primarily responsible for increasing and decreasing the size of the thoracic cavity, age-related muscular changes are extremely important in regulating the amount of air actually in the lungs.

3. The lungs become less elastic with age, thus reducing vital capacity, which is the maximum amount of air that can be expelled from the lungs after a full inspiration. Residual volume, or the amount of air left in the lungs during respiration, increases with age, leaving less air available for oxygen-carbon dioxide exchange.

4. A decrease in numbers of capillaries surrounding the alveoli and an increase in the thickness of the alveolar and capillary membranes occurs with age. Diffusing capacity, or the transfer of air from the alveoli and carbon dioxide from the capillary blood, is lessened. These changes probably help cause the greater fatigability of older persons.

Implications of Age-Related Changes in the Respiratory System

Even though age-related changes occur in the respiratory system, they usually do not handicap older persons unduly in the performance of normal daily activities. It is only when strain, stress, or disease is imposed on the system that age-related change becomes significant for adaptive behavior. As is true in so many of the body systems, most individuals have enough reserve capacity to be able to tolerate some degree of reduced organ efficiency without producing substantial or even noticeable limitations in their behavior.

For most people, respiratory efficiency may be retained well into older age by regular systematic exercise designed to promote muscle tone and by the maintenance of general physical fitness. Stress situations accentuate the reduced system efficiency associated with aging, while exercise and physical fitness serve to at least partially offset the impact of the aging process.

Age-Related Disorders of the Respiratory System

According to most authorities, the respiratory system is affected by the same diseases in both young and old, but symptoms may differ in older people so that pathology can be easily overlooked or diagnosed too late for the most effective treatment.

Pulmonary Tuberculosis

Tuberculosis is an infectious disease that may attack any organ system or tissue of the body, but most deaths occur from tuberculosis of the lungs. The total number of persons with tuberculosis has declined in recent years; however, the highest incidence of occurrence has now shifted to the elderly population. In the older age group this disease does not usually begin as a new infection but as a reactivation of a long dormant tuberculosis infection. Persons who are old, debilitated, and with lowered resistance are more likely to become reinfected. Symptoms develop gradually and the disease may be far advanced before it is identified. Modern chemotherapeutic treatment techniques are usually successful.

Lung Cancer

Lung cancer occurs more frequently among the elderly than among the young and often coexists with chronic lung disease. Factors influencing development of lung cancers are smoking, occupational hazards such as dust, asbestos, or pollution, and chronic lung tissue damage. Treatment is minimally successful so prevention should be given high priority.

Chronic Obstructive Pulmonary Disease

Bronchitis.   This is an inflammation of the bronchi, causing swelling, mucous secretion, and interference with the flow of air in and out of the lungs. It is associated with recurring lung infections and may become chronic.

Emphysema.   Emphysema refers to the breakdown of the alveolar walls in the lungs. Functionally, the lungs lose the ability to stretch and relax, thus remaining partially filled with stale, oxygen-poor air. The incidence of emphysema increases with age and by 90 most persons are likely to have some signs of this disease. According to a brochure published in 1975 by the American Lung Association, emphysema and chronic bronchitis deaths have increased 900 percent in the past 30 years.

Asthma.   This is an allergic condition in which the airway narrows.

Bronchitis, emphysema, and asthma make up the classification referred to as chronic obstructive pulmonary disease. Causes are combinations of environmental and genetic factors. Treatment is usually continual and includes drugs, respiratory therapy, breathing exercises, and the avoidance of respiratory infections, smoking, pollution, and other irritants. Since breathing is so crucial to life, persons with respiratory disease often become fearful, anxious, and demanding. Psychological support, education, and the encouragement of independence are recommended adjuncts to medical treatment.

Pneumonia

A disease responsible for countless deaths prior to the discovery of antibiotics, pneumonia remains a major cause of death among the elderly. Aspiration of foreign materials, decrease in lung functioning, poor circulation, and susceptibility to infection may all lead to pneumonia. Lobar pneumonia (inflammation of the lobes of the lungs) is less common in the elderly than bronchopneumonia (inflammation of the bronchi). Symptoms are not always obvious among the elderly and may go unnoticed or may be misinterpreted until the disease is advanced. Antibiotics and respiratory therapy are used in treatment.

SUMMARY

Diseases of the respiratory system are often progressive and debilitating. Prevention is the best cure and should include avoiding irritants such as smoking, pollution, hair spray, dust, and so forth; correct posture; adequate diet; weight reduction or control; avoiding respiratory infections; and proper breathing.

BIBLIOGRAPHY

Books

American Lung Association. *What Everyone Should Know About Emphysema.* Greenfield, Mass.: Channing L. Bete Co., 1975.

Freeman, E. The respiratory system. In Brocklehurst, J.C., ed., *Textbook of Geriatric Medicine and Gerontology.* Edinburgh and London: Churchill Livingstone, 1973.

Hodkinson, H.M. *An Outline of Geriatrics.* New York: Academic Press, 1975.

Klocke, Robert A. Influence of aging on the lung. In Finch, Caleb E. and Hayflick, Leonard, eds., *Handbook of the Biology of Aging.* New York: Van Nostrand Reinhold, 1977.

Macey, Robert. *Human Physiology,* 2nd ed. Englewood Cliffs, N.J.: Prentice-Hall, 1973.

Petty, Thomas L. Chronic respiratory diseases. In Steinberg, Franz., ed., *Cowdry's the Care of the Geriatric Patient.* 5th ed. St. Louis: Mosby, 1976.

Unit 9

The Digestive System

The human digestive system is composed essentially of the alimentary canal and several accessory organs and glands. The alimentary canal is a hollow tube with openings at both ends—the mouth, where food enters the body, and the anus, where waste material is expelled. The canal is about 15 feet long in the adult body, so that many folds and convolutions are necessary for it to fit into the average human torso.

The organs that make up the alimentary canal, plus several accessory organs and glands, act mechanically and chemically to alter the form of food taken into the body. Through the process of digestion, food is converted into nutritive substances that are absorbed into the bloodstream and delivered to body cells to provide the fuel needed for life processes to be maintained.

The components of the digestive system are organized into two divisions:

1 . The alimentary canal, which consists of:
   Mouth, teeth, and tongue
   Pharynx
   Esophagus
   Stomach
   Small intestine (duodenum, jejunum, ileum)
   Large intestine (cecum, colon, rectum)

2. Accessory glands and organs
   Salivary glands
   Liver
   Pancreas
   Gallbladder

DIGESTION

The Mouth

When food enters the mouth, saliva is secreted by the salivary glands. The secretion of saliva is primarily a reflexive activity although it is conditioned to some extent by learned experiences. For example, think of some food you like and your mouth will probably "water"; the thought alone is sufficient to trigger a salivation response. Two or three pints of saliva are produced each day. Some of the significant functions of saliva are:

1. To moisten and lubricate mouth surfaces and thus aid in both speech and swallowing.
2. To partially dissolve food and thus to stimulate the taste buds.
3. To lubricate food so it can be swallowed more easily.
4. To initiate the digestive process through direct action of enzymes contained in saliva.
5. To act as a cleanser for the mouth cavity and teeth.

The Pharynx and the Esophagus

In addition to being partly dissolved by saliva, solid or semisolid food in the mouth must be chewed and pulverized into a form that can be swallowed. In the act of swallowing, food of a suitable size is pushed back toward the throat by the tongue into the pharynx, the common passageway for both food and air. Once food reaches the pharynx, the act of swallowing becomes involuntary and is no longer under conscious control. The pharynx contracts when food enters it, forcing food substances into the esophagus. The position of the tongue during the first stage of swallowing prevents food from returning to the mouth. Food does not pass into the nasal cavity because the soft palate moves up to block off the cavity, nor does it enter the larynx or the respiratory passage as the muscles of the larynx seal off the laryngeal opening. At this time the vocal cords draw tightly together and during the act of swallowing respiration is inhibited. Thus, food has but one place to go—into the esophagus and stomach.

Food then moves down the esophagus by the force of peristalsis or rhythmic muscular contractions and relaxations which literally push it through the tube. Most food passes from the mouth to the stomach in 6 or 7 seconds. At the junction of the esophagus and stomach is a circular muscle that opens, allowing food to enter the stomach.

The Stomach

The stomach is not as large as most people think and in the empty state appears similar to a deflated balloon. Fortunately

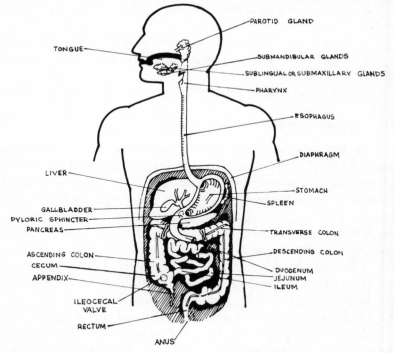

Figure 8. The digestive system.

for those who enjoy eating, the stomach can and does expand (within limits) depending on the amount of food delivered to it.

It is estimated that there are 30 to 40 million gastric glands in the stomach and the juices they secrete continue digestion begun by the salivary glands in the mouth. Many of the gastric glands secrete acid, for a certain amount of acid is necessary in normal gastrointestinal functioning. While this chemical activity is taking place, food continues to be pushed through the stomach by peristaltic movements that churn, pulverize, and thoroughly mix it with gastric juices.

At the lower end of the stomach is the pyloric sphincter, a muscle that separates the stomach from the small intestine and functions as an effective strainer. It usually allows liquids to pass through first, carbohydrates next, then proteins and fats (the hardest and slowest to digest). The emptying of stomach contents into the duodenum, the first section of the small intestine, is a gradual process usually completed after 3 to 5 hours.

Emotional states such as excitement, fear, anger, or grief inhibit gastric motility and alter glandular secretions. As a result, proper digestion may be impaired by either severe or long-term emotional stress.

The Small Intestine

The small intestine is a coiled tube connecting the stomach with the large intestine. Anatomically, the inner surface of the tube is lined with finger-like projections called "villi." Actual digestion of food occurs principally in the small intestine rather than in the stomach. Food moves through the small intestine by strong peristaltic activity, while other rhythmical movements churn and mix the food with glandular secretions to facilitate absorption by the numerous villi.

Digestion in the small intestine depends upon the liver's secretion of bile, usually stored in the gallbladder until needed by the small intestine; the presence of enzymes secreted by the pancreas; and the presence of intestinal juices. All of these substances participate in the breakdown of food so it can be absorbed by the blood and delivered to body cells for immediate use. The undigested part of the food passes into the large intestine as residue or waste material to be excreted from the body in the form of feces.

The Large Intestine

Anatomically, the large intestine is about five feet long, is not arranged in folds as is the small intestine, nor does it have villi on the interior surface. The first portion of the large intestine, the cecum, is a blind pouch from which projects a narrow tube called the appendix (on the right side of the body). Rupture of the appendix is especially dangerous because waste material is expelled directly into the body cavity resulting in dangerous inflammation or peritonitis.

Food residue enters the large intestine from the small intestine through the ileocecal valve. In the large intestine, the residue is subjected to strong muscle action, which carries the residue (feces) to the lower part of the large intestine, or colon, where periodically it passes into the rectum and is expelled through the anus. Defecation is a reflexive act initiated by the accumulation of feces in the rectum. Voluntary control of the anal sphincter muscles is absolutely required for social acceptability. One of the most devastating assaults on self-image is to experience partial or total loss of control over bladder or bowels.

Defecation habits vary greatly among individuals and it is of practical importance in gerontological education to recognize that such substantial variation is common and normal. "Regularity" does not require one bowel movement a day as the advertising media imply; every other day, once a week or possibly even longer intervals may be "regular" patterns for many healthy persons. Individual biological systems, exercise or lack of it, the type and bulk of foods consumed, and emotional status all affect intestinal activity. Taking a laxative once a day may do more harm than good as such a practice easily fosters medicinal dependency. Dependence on laxatives leads to sluggishness of the intestinal musculature and the need for continued artificial stimulation. Such unnecessary dependence very likely sets the stage for the development of future serious gastrointestinal problems. Exercise, proper diet, and reduced stress aid regularity in the normal system no matter what one's age. These factors are especially important, however, in older age.

Age-Related Changes in the Digestive System

Changes in the Mouth

Age-related changes in the mouth include a) a decrease in the number of taste buds on the tongue; b) a decrease in the secretion of the salivary and digestive glands, especially in the amount of ptyalin and amylase secreted; c) an increase in the thickness of mucin (the main component of mucus); d) more alkaline saliva; and e) some shrinking of bony structures.

Throughout life the mouth is exposed to continual trauma that may eventually accentuate or produce age-related changes and/or disease. It is thus very difficult to determine the difference between pathology of the mouth and normal age-related changes.

Changes in the Esophagus

Changes in the esophagus include a) a decrease in peristalsis (contraction and relaxation); and b) a delay in emptying contents due to less frequent openings of the sphincter muscle in the lower esophagus.

Changes in the Stomach

These include a) reduced gastric motility caused by loss of muscle tone and resulting in delays in stomach emptying; b) reduction in stomach volume; c) shrinkage of mucous membranes in the stomach; d) a decline in the number of gastric cells; and e) reduction in the secretion of both hydrochloric acid and enzymes, hindering the breakdown and absorption of nutrients.

Changes in the Intestines

Changes in the intestines include a) decreased tone of intestinal muscle which may slow peristalsis; b) loss of elasticity of abdominal muscles, contributing to constipation; c) shrinking of the mucous lining and a decline in the number of absorbing cells.

Other Changes

Due to thicker and smaller amounts of bile produced, the gallbladder may not empty easily.

The alveolar structures (small sacs) of the pancreas undergo deterioration with some likelihood of occlusion of the ducts.

Thus, although it is possible to cite a substantial number of age-related changes in the digestive system, the functional significance of such changes does not seem to be too great. Basically, digestive processes become slower and somewhat less efficient, but the system remains adequate to meet most reasonable demands imposed on it.

Age-Related Disorders of the Digestive System

Disorders of the Mouth

Older persons represent an age group in which multiple problems of the mouth are seen. These are usually the consequence of poor dental hygiene, decayed teeth, decrease in salivary secretion, poor nutrition, or ill-fitting dentures, partial plates, or bridges. Many lesions in the lips and mouth are caused by chronic irritation as from a pipe, a jagged or sharp tooth, or

a bridge. Since pain is usually not present, lesions may go unnoticed.

*Leukoplakia (white patches on the mucous
membrane).* Leukoplakia is a precancerous lesion also commonly found in older adults and, when observed, should be
treated immediately. Any sore in the mouth, especially one that
bleeds, has irregular edges, and is raised should be inspected by
a doctor or dentist.

Peridontal Disease. Poor nutrition is closely related to
dental caries and *peridontal* (around the teeth) *disease.* Regular
dental checkups are important throughout life irrespective of
whether the individual has dentures or natural teeth.

Hiatus Hernia

Hiatus hernia is a condition common to the elderly,
especially obese older women, in which a small portion of the
stomach slides up through the opening where the esophagus
passes through the diaphragm. Probable causes include muscle
weakness around the diaphragmatic opening, kyphosis (hunchback), scoliosis (lateral curvature of the spine), and straining
during bowel movements. This problem may be present for
years with few symptoms, but symptoms often tend to occur
when bending over, lying flat, or overeating. Heartburn,
regurgitation, belching, difficulty in swallowing, and chest pain
that is easily confused with a heart attack are the usual in-
dicators; however, indigestion may also frequently be a symptom indicative of hiatus hernia in the elderly. This condition is
usually treated nonsurgically unless it becomes severe.

Peptic Ulcer

A peptic ulcer is an erosion of the wall of the stomach or
duodenum. The peak incidence of ulcer formation occurs in
middle age, but new ulcers can develop in older people as well.

Symptoms may be vague and atypical in the elderly; therefore, unusual weight loss, general debility, anemia, abdominal distress, nausea, and vomiting should always be regarded as suspicious signs and possibly indicative of peptic ulcer.

Diverticulosis

A "blind pocket," pouch, or sac in the intestines (especially in the colon) caused by weakness of the abdominal wall is referred to as diverticulosis. If this becomes inflamed and infected, *diverticulitis* results. Pain, nausea, abdominal discomfort, and changes in bowel functions may indicate diverticulitis. Treatment is conservative except when severe complications such as rupture of the diverticuli occur.

Carcinoma

The incidence of cancer of the esophagus increases with age, especially in the seventh and eighth decades, and is more prevalent among men. A disease of middle and late life, cancer of the stomach has a high mortality rate due to early spread of the disease before symptoms appear. The intestinal tract is the second leading site of cancer in the body. Symptoms are not always specific or present, but may include changes in bowel functioning, bowel obstruction, loss of weight, and poor appetite. Pain is often not present until the later stages of the disease. Surgery, usually indicated, may or may not be successful, depending upon when treatment is begun. Cancer of the gallbladder and liver are quite rare, but cancer in the pancreas occurs with increasing frequency among persons over age 50.

Gallbladder Disease

The incidence of gallbladder inflammation and gallstone formation increases with age. Gallstones are formed around insoluble substances in the bile. Symptoms may be minimal or nonexistent unless the "stones" block the duct or move around in the duct. Pain is the primary symptom as well as nausea, vomiting, and inability to digest fatty foods. Attacks tend to increase in number and severity.

BIBLIOGRAPHY

Books

Abbey, June C. Digestive disorders in the aged. In Burnside, Irene M., ed., *Nursing and the Aged.* New York: McGraw-Hill, 1976.

Agate, John. *The Practice of Geriatrics,* 2nd ed. Springfield, Ill.: Charles C Thomas, 1970.

Bhanthumnavin, Kowit and Schuster, Marvin M. Aging and gastrointestinal function. In Finch, Caleb E. and Hayflick, Leonard, eds., *Handbook of the Biology of Aging.* New York: Van Nostrand Reinhold, 1977.

Brocklehurst, J.C. The large bowel. In Brocklehurst, J.C., ed., *Textbook of Geriatric Medicine and Gerontology.* Edinburgh and London: Churchill Livingstone, 1973.

Hodkinson, H.M. *An Outline of Geriatrics.* New York: Academic Press, 1975.

Leeming, J.T., Webster, S.P.G. and Dymock, I.W. The upper gastrointestinal tract, small bowel and exocrine pancreas. In Brocklehurst, J.C., ed., *Textbook of Geriatric Medicine and Gerontology.* Edinburgh and London: Churchill Livingstone, 1973.

Strauss, B. Disorders of the digestive system. In Rossman, I., ed., *Clinical Geriatrics.* Philadelphia: Lippincott, 1971.

Periodicals

Berman, P.M. and Kirsner, J.B. The aging gut. II. Diseases of the colon, pancreas, liver and gallbladder, functional bowel disease and iatrogenic disease. *Geriatrics 27:*117, 1972.

Harant, Z. and Goldberger, J.V. Treatment of anemia in the aged: a common problem and challenge. *Journal of the American Geriatrics Society 23:*127, 1975.

Kampmann, J.P., Sinding, J. and Moller-Jorgensen. Effects of age on liver function. *Geriatrics 30:*91, 1975.

Painter, N.S. Diverticular disease of the colon: a bane of the elderly. *Geriatrics 31:*89, 1976.

Unit 10

The Urinary System

The urinary system includes two kidneys, two ureters, the bladder, and the urethra. This body system interacts with other organs of excretion, the lungs, skin, and intestines, to maintain the homeostatic equilibrium necessary for the maintenance of life.

The primary functions of the urinary system are to:

1. Excrete the toxic substances and waste products of metabolism.
2. Regulate water balance in the body.
3. Help maintain the acid-base equilibrium in body fluids.
4. Aid in controlling the concentration of salts and other necessary substances in the blood.

THE KIDNEYS

The kidneys are paired, bean-shaped organs situated behind the abdominal cavity and slightly below the diaphragm, but outside the peritoneum, the membrane enclosing the abdominal cavity. In the average adult, each kidney is about five inches long.

The basic unit of the kidney is the *nephron,* in which urine formation and the other life maintaining activities of the kidneys take place. Each kidney contains about one million nephrons. A nephron consists of a renal corpuscle composed of a glomerulus—a coiled series of small blood capillaries enclosed in a capsule—and a renal tubule. The blood is carried from the renal artery to the capillaries in the glomerulus, an anatomical

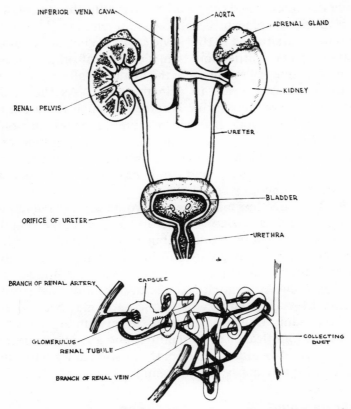

Figure 9. The urinary system and the blood supply of the nephron.

arrangement that provides a rich blood supply to the nephron. The water and minerals taken out of the blood by the glomerulus pass successively through renal tubules, collecting tubules, renal pelvis, ureters, bladder, and urethra.

It is estimated we can lose about 60 percent of the two million nephrons in the kidneys before blood chemistry is significantly impaired. Humans are able to live successfully with only one functioning kidney.

Contractions of the smooth muscle walls of the ureters connecting the kidneys and the bladder force urine into the bladder. The bladder, where urine is collected and temporarily stored, is a muscular sac situated in the pelvic cavity. When approximately 300 milliliters (a little more than a cupful) of urine collects in the bladder, sensory receptors in the bladder wall are stimulated and the conscious desire to urinate results. As the bladder sphincter muscles relax, urine is forced through the urethra to the outside of the body (the act of urination or micturition).

The urethra is short and exclusively excretory in females. In males it extends from the bladder through the penis, carries both urine and semen, and thus has both excretory and reproductive functions.

Bladder function may be either voluntary or involuntary, depending upon a variety of factors. For example, children must be taught bladder control, but it is not until the child is physically mature enough to be able to voluntarily withhold urine that toilet training can be accomplished. Although normally controllable, in situations of extreme emotional stress or excitement loss of voluntary bladder control may occur even in the normal adult. Urination is essentially a voluntary act, one of tremendous significance in our culture, and any loss or decreased efficiency of bladder functioning (as sometimes happens in older age) is particularly embarrassing.

Kidney Functions

The kidneys maintain the constancy of blood in the body by removing excess quantities of various materials from the blood and excreting these as urine. Urine consists of about 95 percent water and 5 percent solids (organic and inorganic materials). Substances found in urine are similar to those in blood.

Urine formation depends upon two complicated processes:

1. *Filtration.* In the nephrons large quantities of water and minerals are filtered from the blood capillaries (the glomeruli) into the renal tubules. Blood pressure provides the force for this

filtration process. Proteins and blood cells are too large to pass into the renal tubules and thus do not normally appear in urine.

2. *Reabsorption* and *tubular secretion.* Fluid in the renal tubules passes on to the collecting ducts, the renal pelvis, and then into the ureters. Fluid composition changes, though, as it passes through the renal tubules, where many substances are reabsorbed through the tubule walls back into the blood (reabsorption) surrounding the tubules. Among the substances that are reabsorbed into the blood from the tubules are water, glucose, chloride, and sodium, which can be used again and again. A few substances, however, are transported in the other direction, from blood capillaries back into the tubular fluid (tubular secretion). The fluid that finally enters the ureters is called *urine.*

Reabsorption is an especially important process in urine formation and illustrates one of the elaborate conservation mechanisms of the human body. For example, under average conditions, about 120 milliliters (ml) of filtered fluid enters the renal tubules each minute, but only about 1 ml of fluid leaves the tubules as urine. More than 99 percent of the fluid (mostly water) is reabsorbed by the blood to be used again. Filtration, reabsorption, and tubular secretion constitute highly efficient processes for water conservation in the body.

The analysis of urine (urinalysis) is a simple but valuable diagnostic tool as it can indicate disease by the presence of substances not normally found in urine or by alterations in the proportions of substances that are normally found.

When the kidneys stop functioning properly, three potentially dangerous situations occur:

1. The level of waste products in the blood increases.

2. Acidity of the blood increases as excess acid is no longer removed by the kidneys.

3. Salt and water balances, both crucial for life, are disrupted and produce serious disequilibrium of the internal environment.

Age-Related Changes in the Urinary System

As in other body systems, the aging process appears to result in reduced efficiency of the kidneys, but not in actual breakdown of their functions. The following changes have been reported as age-related phenomena in the urinary system:

Decrease in Nephrons

Nephrons, the basic functional units of the kidneys, decrease in number with age. Evidence suggests that a 75-year-old individual has probably lost from one-third to one-half of his/her original two million nephrons and that the remaining nephrons will undergo gradual and progressive degenerative changes. Such changes imply a) a decrease in filtration rate. For example, the kidneys of an average 30-year-old person filter approximately 120 ml of blood per minute, while the kidneys of an average 75-year-old person filter about 60 ml of blood per minute; b) a gradual decrease in both the excretory and the reabsorptive functions of the renal tubules; and c) a more easily disrupted acid-base balance of the body due to decreasing efficiency of the urinary system. Any sudden loss or deprivation of fluid such as would result from diarrhea, vomiting, decrease in cardiac output, or not drinking enough water (common in older persons) is more likely to result in serious renal insufficiency in older individuals than in the young.

Decrease in Renal Blood Flow

Renal blood flow is reduced with age because the entire arterial tree supplying the kidneys with blood gradually becomes physically smaller. At age 20, one-fourth of the blood pumped by the heart circulates through the kidneys; at 80, it is estimated that only one-eighth of the blood pumped from the heart reaches the kidneys.

Loss of Muscle Tone in Urinary Structures

The ureters, bladder, and urethra are all muscular structures and tend to lose tone and elasticity with age. The bladder may be especially affected as a decrease in muscle tone leads to incomplete emptying of the bladder, with the consequent greater risk of infections.

Declining Bladder Capacity

Total bladder capacity declines with age from approximately 500 to 600 ml to about 250 ml. Lessened capacity plus weaker muscle tone contributes to more frequent and also more urgent urination in many older persons. In addition, the need or signal to urinate may be delayed until the bladder is almost full, resulting in even greater urgency.

Urinary incontinence becomes a problem for some of the elderly. Anyone working with this age group must be aware that such difficulties can be acutely embarrassing in our culture which is especially sensitive about the control of all excretory activities. Even partial urinary incontinence may be a serious psychological and social handicap sometimes leading to increasing disengagement and withdrawal from social activities as well as to reduced interpersonal relationships because of fear of embarrassment and possible rejection. An awareness of the significant emotional implications of urinary system changes and sensitivity to them is essential. For example, planned frequent rest breaks during trips or programs make participation more comfortable and pleasurable for all, but especially for the elderly who are more easily stressed by any type of endurance activity.

Physical exercise designed to promote and maintain muscle tone is suggested as one way of preventing or reducing age-related incontinence. For more difficult problems, bowel and bladder training is generally successful in restoring adequate control over excretory functions (21). Rehabilitative gains from such measures include better physical control as well as a feeling of mastery over a situation perceived as personally and socially humiliating.

Age-related changes in the urinary system result in reduced efficiency due to a loss of reserve capacity, not in the inability of the system to function adequately in normal situations.

Age-Related Disorders of the Urinary System

Medical problems involving the urinary system stem from the progressive decrease in renal function and renal blood supply with age, a greater likelihood of obstruction in the lower urinary tract, and increased susceptibility to infection. Urinary tract infections may be extremely persistent, difficult to control, and even more difficult to cure.

Urinary Tract Infections

Cystitis.   This is an inflammation of the bladder found frequently in older persons, especially in women since the short urethra makes the female bladder more accessible to bacteria. Symptoms include urgency and frequency of urination, lower abdominal pain, burning or pain on urinating and sometimes blood in the urine. Whether or not this infection is curable depends upon its severity and the effectiveness of the prescribed treatment.

Pyelonephritis.   Pyelonephritis is caused by one of several types of bacteria and is a serious form of urinary tract infection that may lead to structural damage of the kidneys, uremia, and progressive renal failure. The course of the disease may be prolonged depending on the cause and on response to treatment. Although observed commonly in older men, older women are also susceptible to this disease. Symptoms include pain in the region of the kidneys, fever, chills, fatigue, weight loss, and gastrointestinal disturbance.

Renal Insufficiency

In the elderly, renal insufficiency, or loss of kidney function, may be due to primary disease of the kidneys or to malfunctioning in other organs, especially the circulatory system. Because of the large reserve functional capacity of the kidneys, renal insufficiency by itself is not considered to be a highly serious problem until at least two-thirds of the kidneys are destroyed.

Uremia

Uremia (chronic renal failure) is due to the retention of certain substances in the blood that the kidneys fail to excrete. It may result from decreased blood flow to the kidneys, which in turn interferes with glomerular filtration rate; or from obstruction of urinary output so that kidney function is impaired by back pressure on the kidneys; or from disease of the kidney itself. Adequate fluid intake is extremely important in older persons since this helps prevent dehydration, which may have serious consequences for this age group.

Prostate Enlargement

Males possess a small prostate gland which is thought to function in the activation of sperm. The prostate surrounds the urethra at the neck of the bladder and if prostate enlargement occurs, urine flow may be painful, reduced, or in some instances completely obstructed. Enlargement is a common occurrence among aging males although the cause is not definitely known. Partial obstruction over time may lead to incomplete bladder emptying, infection, back pressure on the kidneys, and other undesirable consequences. Surgery is usually the prescribed treatment.

Carcinoma

The prostate and the bladder are the most common sites of cancers in the urinary system. Cancer of the prostate occurs most often in the elderly, but bladder cancer is also reported more frequently in males after age 50. Cigarette smoking or exposure to certain chemicals may be causative factors. Early diagnosis improves chances of recovery.

BIBLIOGRAPHY

Books

Agate, John. *The Practice of Geriatrics,* 2nd ed. Springfield, Ill.: Charles C Thomas, 1970.

Goldman, Ralph. Aging of the excretory system: kidney and bladder. In Finch, Caleb E. and Hayflick, Leonard, eds., *Handbook of the Biology of Aging.* New York: Van Nostrand Reinhold, 1977.

Lindeman, Robert D. Age changes in renal function. In Goldman, Ralph and Rockstein, Morris, eds., *The Physiology and Pathology of Human Aging.* New York: Academic Press, 1975.

Sourander, L.B. Genito-urinary system. In Brocklehurst, J.C., ed., *Textbook of Geriatric Medicine and Gerontology.* Edinburgh and London: Churchill Livingstone, 1975.

Periodicals

Burch, G.E. The senile kidneys. *American Heart Journal 88:*259, 1974.

Kent, S. The intimate relationship between the urinary system and the sexual function. *Geriatrics 30:*138, 1975.

Owen, W.L. Cancer of the prostate: a literature review. *Journal of Chronic Diseases 29:*89, 1976.

Parsons, V. What decreasing renal function means to aging patients. *Geriatrics 32:*93, 1977.

Prout, G.R. and Paulson, D.F. The inevitable prostate problem. *Medical World News 15:*27, 1974.

Wear, J.B. Solving selected problems of the aging urinary tract. *Postgraduate Medicine 58:*179, 1975.

Whitehead, J.A. Urinary incontinence in the aged. *Geriatrics 22:*154, 1967.

Unit 11

The Reproductive System

The male and female reproductive systems are composed of both internal and external organs.

COMPONENTS AND FUNCTIONS OF THE FEMALE REPRODUCTIVE SYSTEM

The external female reproductive organs include:

● The external genitalia or *vulva,* made up of the labia majora, labia minora, clitoris, vestibule, and hymen.

● *Mammary glands* (breasts), composed of a nipple, lobes (15 or 20 arranged radially within fat), connective tissue, and excretory ducts. These glands respond to estrogen, progesterone, and prolactin by increasing and decreasing in size and by secreting milk.

The internal organs include:

● The *vagina,* a tubular canal forming the birth passageway and functioning as the organ of copulation.

● The *uterus,* a muscular, pear-shaped organ suspended in front of the rectum and situated above the bladder. Four sets of ligaments hold the uterus in place.

● *Ovaries,* two almond-shaped organs about one-and-a-half inches long lying on either side of the uterus near the fallopian tubes. The ovaries are the primary organs of reproduction in the female. Their functions are to develop and release mature ova and to produce the hormones estrogen and progesterone.

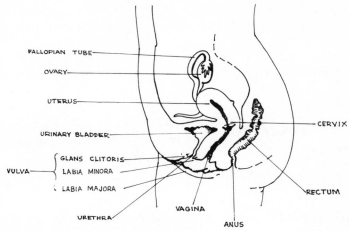

Figure 10. Female reproductive system.

Age-Related Changes in the Female Reproductive System

One phenomenon of aging that is consistent in females is the loss of reproductive capacity (climacteric).

1. Usually occurring between the ages of 42 and 52, the climacteric marks the end of menstruation and coincides with the cessation of reproductive ability. Decreased amounts of estrogen and progesterone are produced by the ovaries at this time, but the adrenal glands usually continue to secrete small amounts of estrogen so that physical changes in the reproductive system are generally gradual and not dramatic.

2. The external genitalia shrink somewhat and there is a decrease in pubic hair.

3. The vaginal canal becomes pale, dry, thin, and less elastic. Glandular secretions in the canal decrease and pH is less acidic.

4. The ovaries and uterus decrease in size and the latter becomes more fibrous.

5. Ligaments supporting these structures tend to lose elasticity.

6. Muscle and glandular tone diminish and skin is less elastic, resulting in a loss of firmness of the breast and other body tissue.

Age-Related Disorders of the Female Reproductive System

Vaginal Problems

These include inflammation and infection of the vagina as well as painful intercourse. Such problems may be caused by a more basic pH and by estrogen depletion. The latter may be improved by estrogen applied locally or taken orally.

Cystocele, Rectocele, Prolapsed Uterus

A herniation into the anterior or posterior vaginal walls (cystocele and rectocele, respectively) frequently causes difficulties in older women. This is particularly true for those who have stretched tissues as a result of childbirth. A feeling of heaviness in the pelvic area accompanied by difficulty in urination or defecation are common complaints. Prolapse of the uterus is the downward displacement of the uterus due to the stretching of tissues during childbirth, and may be slight or severe. Surgery is the treatment of choice for all of the above disorders.

Benign Tumors

Nonmalignant tumors often develop in the uterus, cervix, vagina, or ovaries. Tumors arising from the muscle of the uterus occur in 20 to 30 percent of all women and may or may not produce symptoms.

Malignancies

Cancer of the vulva is most commonly seen in elderly women. About 50 percent of the cases are accompanied by thick and shiny white patches (leukoplakia) and approximately two-thirds of the women who have this disease complain of itching and pruritus. Any vaginal discharge or bleeding can be an indication of a malignancy of the vagina, cervix, or uterus. Unfortunately, ovarian tumors are sometimes malignant and far advanced before treatment is begun. It is therefore very important that regular gynecological examinations be continued even into old age.

Cancer of the breast is a leading cause of death in older women. While some changes in breast tissue are benign, all should be viewed as suspicious until diagnosis is made. A monthly breast self-examination is of utmost importance to every woman no matter how old. When discovered early, cure rates for breast malignancy are significantly higher than when cancer has spread into the lymph tissue.

COMPONENTS AND FUNCTIONS OF THE MALE REPRODUCTIVE SYSTEM

The external organs of the male consist of:

● The *scrotum,* suspended from the pubis (front section of the pelvis), which encloses and supports the testes.

● The *penis,* composed of erectile tissue, functions as the organ of copulation and excretion.

The internal organs include:

● The *testes,* significant in the production of spermatozoa (sperm cells) and the secretion of the male sex hormones, including testosterone. These hormones influence the appearance of secondary sex characteristics, the development of the body, and behavior.

● A *system of ducts* transmits the spermatozoa from the testes to the outside of the body. These include the epididymis, which is continuous with the ductus deferens and merges with the seminal vesicle ducts ending in the ejaculatory duct. The latter duct ejects semen containing spermatozoa and various glandular fluids into the urethra, which carries both semen and urine.

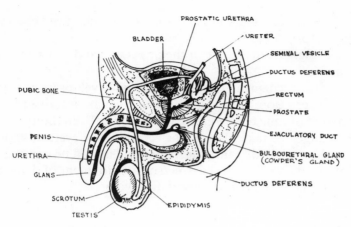

Figure 11. Male reproductive system.

● The *prostate gland* surrounds the section of the urethra near the bladder and secretes an alkaline fluid thought to activate spermatozoa in the urethra.

● Two *Cowper's glands,* each about the size of a pea, lie on either side of the urethra and below the prostate. These secrete a clear, mucous-like substance in the urethra that becomes part of the semen and acts as a lubricant.

● The two *seminal vesicles* lie near the lower surface of the bladder and secrete a thick fluid that mixes with the sperm from the testes.

Age-Related Changes in the Male Reproductive System

The male climacteric usually occurs between ages 48 and 60 and is not as identifiable as is the female climacteric. The main changes that occur are:

1. Testosterone levels decline, resulting in a decrease in the size and firmness of the testes and more dense seminiferous tubules.

2. Fewer sperm are produced and sexual energy lessens somewhat.

3. The amount and consistency of the seminal fluid changes and ejaculatory force is diminished.

4. An increase in the size of the prostate gland often accompanies aging.

5. Sexual excitement during stimulation develops more slowly as does an erection, although an erection can be sustained for a longer period of time before ejaculation occurs. Even though age-related changes do take place in the reproductive system, sexual activity need not significantly decrease, but should be continued as an important part of an older person's enjoyment of living as well as serving as a mark of continuing vigor.

SEXUALITY

Although stereotypes and myths about the sexual needs of older adults abound, Masters and Johnson (22) have reported that persons who remain in reasonably good health should be able to continue satisfying sexual activity well into old age. The sexual responses of the aging male and female change, but the changes complement one another. For instance, men over 60 tend to be aroused and achieve erection more slowly than younger men, but they are also often able to prolong the erection and thus match very adequately the female's decreased response time in the excitement stage of sexual arousal.

Many physical, social, and psychological variables influence sexual expression in older persons. One important variable is the individual's state of health. Heart disease or a heart attack may result in fears concerning ability to engage in sexual intercourse that can prove devastating to both partners, especially to those who have always enjoyed their sexual activity. All members of the helping professions need to be cognizant of the possible ramifications of heart disease on sexuality, and should provide appropriate information, counseling, support, and understanding to these individuals and their spouses.

Another health disorder that may result in inadequate sexual performance in the male is diabetes, as dysfunctioning of nerve cells often occurs when diabetes is not well controlled. Similarly, females who have diabetes sometimes experience frigidity in sexual relations. Other conditions of the female reproductive system such as dryness of the vagina, painful intercourse, prolapse of the uterus, rectocele, and cystocele are likely contributors to unpleasant sexual experiences.

It is not possible to mention here all of the health disorders that can interfere with sexuality, but stroke, arthritis, colostomy, hysterectomy, and breast amputation are examples of health problems that can adversely affect sexual activity. In addition, certain substances taken into the body may impair optimal sexual functioning. Chronic alcoholism, heavy smoking, and the ingestion of certain drugs such as tranquilizers and barbiturates all reduce the sex drive and potency. Realizing that the incidence of health problems increases with age, and that many elders smoke excessively and use drugs and alcohol, helping professionals should be aware of the possible effects of these factors in sexual functioning and should be prepared to assist in the resolution of such problems. The inability to discuss these matters openly with those in the helping professions adds immeasurably to feelings of frustration and failure in the older adult.

Society's response to sexual expression in older age is a potent force in generating sexual problems for this age group. In the past, sexual activity was generally considered to be reserved for the procreation of children and, for women, as something to be endured but not enjoyed. According to this older view, sexual expression in the later years is not an appropriate behavior. In addition, children sometimes view their parents, especially older parents, as sexless, and become upset when a parent expresses interest in dating or remarrying. To further complicate matters, women usually live longer than men; thus widowhood or the unavailability of a partner substantially reduces opportunities for sexual expression in the later years.

All of these physical, social, and psychological factors, as well as others such as overindulgence in food, physical or mental fatigue, fear of sexual failure, preoccupation with a career or other outside interest, signs of aging such as wrinkles and gray hair, or a sexual relationship that is boring or monotonous influence sexual performance and enjoyment in the older person.

For the elderly who are institutionalized there are generally few opportunities for privacy or conjugal visits even though they, too, are concerned about sexuality and have a need for sexual relationships. Wasow and Loeb (23) report that nursing home residents believe sexual intercourse is acceptable for other elderly persons, but that they are not able to participate in sexual activity because of lack of opportunity. Nursing home residents' interests in sex or overt sexual behavior are frequently viewed as aberrant by the staff and may result in ridicule or even punishment. Such inappropriate reactions of staff members and others who work directly with the elderly support the need for continued education in life-span sexuality and the assessment of personal attitudes toward the sexual needs of elders. Without understanding and changes in attitudes, sex will continue to be looked upon as a privilege of the young that is to be denied to the old.

Although patterns of sexual interest and activity vary in males and females through the years, if sexual expression is maintained and is satisfying, the likelihood is that it will continue, and will add to a sense of love, belonging, and security well into older age.

BIBLIOGRAPHY

Books

Anderson, Helen. *Newton's Geriatric Nursing,* 5th ed. St. Louis: Mosby, 1971.

Birchenall, Joan and Streight, Mary E. *Care of the Older Adult.* Philadelphia: Lippincott, 1973.

Boyarsky, Rose. Sexuality. In Steinberg, Franz U., ed., *Cowdry's the Care of the Geriatric Patient,* 5th ed. St. Louis: Mosby, 1976.

Brunner, Lillian S. and Suddarth, Doris S. *Textbook of Medical Surgical Nursing,* 3rd ed. Philadelphia: Lippincott, 1975.

Burnside, Irene M., ed., *Sexuality and Aging.* Los Angeles: University of Southern California Press, 1975.

Goldman, Ralph, Rockstein, Morris and Sussman, Marvin L. *The Physiology and Pathology of Human Aging.* New York: Academic Press, 1975.

Kimmel, Douglas. *Adulthood and Aging.* New York: Wiley, 1974.

Verwoerdt, Adrian. *Clinical Geropsychiatry.* Baltimore: Williams and Wilkins, 1976.

Woodruff, Diana S. and Birren, James F., eds., *Aging: Scientific Perspectives and Social Issues.* New York: Van Nostrand, 1975.

Periodicals

Cameron, Paul and Biber, Henry. Sexual thought throughout the life span. *Gerontologist 13:*144, 1973.

Costello, Marilyn K. Sex, intimacy and aging. *American Journal of Nursing 38:*1330, 1975.

Daw, E. Recent concepts in the treatment of menopausal symptoms. *Practitioner 215:*501, 1975.

Dean, S.R. Geriatric sexuality: normal, needed and neglected. *Geriatrics 29:*134, 1974.

DeNicola, P. and Peruzza, M. Sex in the aged. *Journal of the American Geriatrics Society 22:*380, 1974.

Flint, M. The menopause: reward or punishment? *Psychosomatics 16:*161, 1975.

Kent, S. Impotence: the facts versus the fallacies. *Geriatrics 30:*164, 1975.

Pease, Ruth A. Sexuality in the aging male. *Gerontologist 14:*153, 1974.

Pfeiffer, Eric. Sexuality in the aging individual. *Journal of the American Geriatrics Society 22:*481, 1974.

Unit 12

The Endocrine System

The regulation and integration of bodily activities depend upon both the nervous system and the endocrine system. The endocrine system functions through ductless endocrine glands that secrete chemical substances called hor-mones directly into the blood or lymph.

Because of the complexity of the endocrine system and the sparse amount of information available about endocrine functions as they relate to the aging process, the following discussion will be selective.

Certain chemical substances in the blood play a primary role in controlling hormone secretion. Such substances may be hormones from other glands or, in some cases, nonhormonal chemicals. For example, secretions of the thyroid gland are triggered by hormones produced in the pituitary, the so-called master gland. Blood sugar, however, a nonhormonal substance, triggers hormone production in the pancreas. Sometimes, hormones secreted by Gland B will, when stimulated by hormones from Gland A, in turn exert some control on Gland A's secretions. In ways such as this, the endocrine system contributes significantly to the maintenance of equilibrium (homeostasis) in the body. Endocrine activity is a complicated type of feedback loop in which one action triggers others so that the necessary internal equilibrium may be maintained in spite of constantly varying demands, both internal and external.

The major glands of the endocrine system, their locations, principal hormones, and probable functions are discussed below.

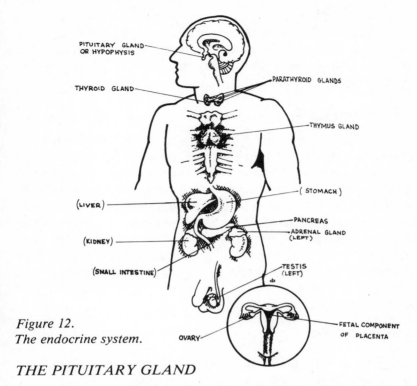

Figure 12.
The endocrine system.

THE PITUITARY GLAND

The pituitary gland is attached to the base of the brain and has two distinct lobes, anterior and posterior. Historically referred to as the "master gland," the pituitary secretes a greater number of different hormones than any other gland in the endocrine system.

The anterior lobe secretes a variety of hormones, including: a) a growth hormone that primarily regulates growth of the body skeleton; b) a thyroid-stimulating hormone that regulates thyroid gland function; c) gonad-stimulating hormones, which are necessary for normal development and functioning of both primary and secondary sex organs; and d) a hormone necessary for the normal development and functioning of the adrenal gland cortex.

The posterior lobe of the pituitary produces two hormones, an antidiuretic hormone (ADH), which is important in controlling water reabsorption in the kidneys, and a hormone that causes uterine contractions during childbirth and stimulates the breasts to release milk after childbirth.

Age-Related Changes and Disorders of the Pituitary Gland

The pituitary gland appears to maintain its overall functioning reasonably well into old age, even though its hormonal secretions generally decline with advancing age. There are no highly significant or well-documented age-related diseases of the pituitary gland, but some better known pituitary disorders (not necessarily related to age) are a) acromegaly, characterized by increased growth in bones of hands, feet, and face; b) Simmonds' disease, which results in premature senility; c) Cushing's syndrome, which is characterized by fatness of the trunk and face; and d) diabetes insipidus, characterized by the excretion of a large volume of urine.

THE THYROID GLAND

The thyroid gland is a two-lobed structure situated on either side of the upper part of the trachea.

The most important hormone produced by the thyroid is thyroxine, a major source of iodine in the body. The thyroid gland assists in the metabolic function of every cell in the body. Energy is produced by oxidative reactions in the cells and the oxidation rate is primarily controlled by the thyroid. An increase in thyroid hormone secretion raises basal metabolic rate, while a decrease in hormone secretion lowers basal metabolic rate.

Age-Related Changes and Disorders of the Thyroid Gland

A gradual decrease in thyroid activity occurs with age, but there is some question as to whether decreased functioning is due exclusively to changes in the thyroid gland or whether it is secondary to changes in the pituitary gland. Common though not necessarily age-related disorders of the thyroid gland include a) goiter, an enlargement of the thyroid because of inadequate iodine intake; b) myxedema, caused by underfunctioning of the thyroid and characterized by low metabolic rate, swelling (edema), rounded features, and loss of hair; c) exophthalmic goiter (Graves' disease) caused by overactivity of the thyroid and characterized by a high metabolic rate, nervous symptoms, protrusion of the eyeballs, and muscular weakness; d) thyroiditis, inflammation of the thyroid gland characterized by painful swelling in the area of the thyroid, difficulty in swallowing, nervousness, loss of weight, and insomnia.

THE PARATHYROID GLANDS

The parathyroid glands are two pairs of small glands located on either side of the thyroid.

Parathyroid hormone is crucial to maintaining adequate blood levels of calcium and phosphorus and, consequently, directly affects the irritability of the nervous system and muscles.

Age-Related Changes and Disorders of the Parathyroid Glands

Aging seems to produce no dramatic change in the parathyroids other than a gradual reduction in glandular activity over time. No age-related disease is known to be specifically associated with the parathyroids; however, the following disorders may sometimes occur in older persons: a) hyperparathyroidism, usually due to an enlargement of the parathyroids and characterized by calcification of the bones and the development of kidney stones containing calcium; and b) hypoparathyroidism, often caused by excessive surgical removal of parathyroid tissue. Tetany (generalized muscle contractions) is the most common manifestation of this disease.

The maintenance of appropriate calcium levels is crucial to

life, and reduced functioning of the parathyroid glands severely affects both nervous and muscle activity.

THE ADRENAL GLANDS

There are two adrenal glands, one located on the upper part of each kidney. Each adrenal gland is composed of two distinct parts, an adrenal cortex (the outer layer) and an adrenal medulla (the central part).

The hormones produced by the adrenal cortex are extremely important in the regulation of salt and water balance (especially sodium and potassium balance), in regulating levels of fats, carbohydrates, and proteins in the body, and in controlling body reactions to stress. Such stresses to the body include extremes of heat or cold, excessive muscular activity, infections, burns, and other types of trauma.

The adrenal medulla plays a significant role in activating responses to emergencies (the "fight or flight" reaction). Its hormones, adrenalin (epinephrine) and norepinephrine, produce the same arousal effects as the sympathetic nervous system, but there are still a number of unresolved questions regarding the role of medullary hormones in humans under normal, non-stressful situations.

Age-Related Changes and Disorders of the Adrenal Glands

Age-related changes involve a gradual reduction in hormonal secretions with age, but whether this is due to changes in the adrenals, pituitary, or other interacting glands is not definitely known. Disorders of the adrenals may occur at any age, but none are known to be clearly related to the aging process. Among the disorders of the adrenal glands that may be observed in older persons are a) Cushing's syndrome, due to hypersecretion of hormones by the adrenal cortex and characterized by a "moon-face," general weakness, fatty deposits around the trunk, and thin legs; b) Addison's disease, resulting from a decrease in the secretion of the adrenal cortex hormones and marked by general weakness, excessive dark pigmentation of the skin, and many other varied symptoms; c) aldosteronism, caused by overproduction of aldosterone by the adrenal glands and characterized by muscle weakness, excessive urination, excessive thirst, hypertension, and other symptoms.

THE PANCREAS

The pancreas is a gland located in front of the first and second lumbar vertebrae and behind the stomach.

The pancreas has two principal functions: a) to secrete digestive juices into the duodenum; and b) to produce and secrete insulin, a major hormone of the endocrine system. It also produces a second hormone, glucagon, which increases the level of glucose in the blood.

Insulin is the most significant regulator of carbohydrate utilization in the body. Along with other hormones it facilitates the use of glucose by body cells, aids in glycogen formation in the liver, and in the conversion of glycogen to glucose, all highly important life-sustaining activities. Insufficient insulin leads to diabetes, characterized by above normal amounts of sugar (glucose) in the blood and urine. Insulin lowers the level of sugar in the blood by promoting the conversion of blood sugar to glycogen in the liver and muscle, by accelerating the use of glucose in the tissues, by slowing the breakdown of fats in the liver, and by slowing the conversion of amino acids to carbohydrates. Too much insulin in the body, however, produces low blood sugar or hypoglycemia. If the level of blood sugar becomes too high or too low, death occurs.

Age-Related Changes and Disorders of the Pancreas

No age-related disease is specifically related to the pancreas; however, diabetes mellitus is extremely common among older adults. Thought to be primarily hereditary, this disease occurs when the cells in the islands of Langerhans of the pancreas fail to secrete adequate amounts of insulin needed to metabolize carbohydrates, resulting in high blood sugar. Obese elderly people seem particularly susceptible to diabetes, but the disease is often mild in this age group. Symptoms are numerous and include excessive thirst, appetite, and urination; weakness; loss of weight; and decreased wound healing. Individuals who have diabetes over a long period of time are likely to develop complications which include generalized arteriosclerosis (hardening of the arteries), damage to the peripheral nerves, and lesions of the extremities that may ulcerate and lead to gangrene. Dietary modification aimed at reducing the intake of carbohydrates, and, if a person is obese, the number of calories, is prescribed along with oral antidiabetes drugs or insulin. Barring severe complications, many older persons are able to live a normal span of years by following the prescribed treatments and by exercising daily.

THE GONADS (TESTES AND OVARIES)

The gonads have a dual role. They produce sperm and ova, the reproductive cells of the body, and also produce hormones. The testes manufacture primarily testosterone, a hormone responsible for the development of secondary sex characteristics in the male as well as growth and development of the penis and scrotum. Estrogens are hormones produced predominantly by the ovaries in the female, although to a degree both sexes produce male and female hormones. Hormone secretion increases at puberty and begins to gradually decrease in middle age. Age-related changes in the gonads are considered in the discussion of the reproductive system.

SUMMARY

Compared with other organ systems of the body, the endocrine glands do not show consistent and predictable age-related changes other than the gradual slowing of functioning. Because of the complex interrelationships between the various endocrine glands, and between the endocrine and nervous systems, specific age-related changes of behavioral significance have not been clearly identified as yet. Diseases associated with endocrine functioning may occur at any age; thus, age-specificity is not a characteristic of the functions of the endocrine system as a whole. Overall, as the various endocrine glands undergo gradual decline in function with age, the ability of the organism to adapt decreases. This constitutes one of the most important and consistent changes associated with the aging process.

BIBLIOGRAPHY

Books

Agate, John. *The Practice of Geriatrics,* 2nd ed. Springfield, Ill.: Charles C Thomas, 1970.

Andres, Reubin and Tobin, Jordan D. Endocrine systems. In Finch, Caleb E. and Hayflick, Leonard, eds., *Handbook of the Biology of Aging.* New York: Van Nostrand Reinhold, 1977.

Gitman, L., ed. *Endocrines and Aging.* Springfield, Ill.: Charles C Thomas, 1967.

Gregerman, R.I. and Bierman, E.L. Aging and hormones. In Williams, R.H., ed., *Textbook of Endocrinology,* 5th ed. Philadelphia: Saunders, 1974.

Hall, M.R.P. Endocrine system. In Brocklehurst, J.C., ed., *Textbook of Geriatric Medicine and Gerontology.* Edinburgh and London: Churchill Livingstone, 1973.

Hodkinson, H.M. *An Outline of Geriatrics,* New York: Academic Press, 1975.

Stahl, Norman L. and Greenblatt, Robert B. Geriatric practice: age and the endocrine system. In Busse, Ewald W., ed., *Theory and Therapeutics of Aging,* New York: Medcom, 1973.

Steen, Edwin B. and Montagu, Ashley. *Anatomy and Physiology.* Vol.2. New York: Barnes and Noble, 1959.

Timiras, P.S. and Meisami, Esmail. Changes in gonadal function. In Timiras, P.S., ed., *Developmental Physiology and Aging.* New York: Macmillan, 1972.

Part III

Unit 13

Homeostasis

Homeostasis is the complex integrated physiologic adjustment of body systems that facilitates the maintenance of a relatively constant environment within the body. The range within which body cells can continue normal life-sustaining activities is rather narrow, and if the range of tolerance is exceeded the organism will die.

Vital body functions such as body temperature, blood pressure, blood sugar, acid-base balance of blood (pH), and sodium, chloride, potassium, and magnesium levels must be maintained within a certain range in order for the organism to continue living. The higher an organism on the evolutionary scale, the more critical homeostatic mechanisms become for survival.

The body has many complex control devices available to help it maintain a "steady state." For example, an increase in blood pressure activates homeostatic control mechanisms to return blood pressure to a normal level so that body functioning is not unduly disturbed. Most, if not all body systems are involved in the continual maintenance of homeostasis, but the nervous and endocrine systems are two of the more crucial systems having integrating and coordinating functions.

Age-related changes occur in all of the organ systems of the human body. Nevertheless, there are large variations in how individuals age and also, within each individual, how the organs age. Barring disease and highly stressful situations, organ

134

systems continue to function adequately well into old age, and the major physical change associated with aging is a loss of reserve capacity in the various systems of the body. The impact of aging, then, occurs most dramatically under conditions of stress when body reserves are needed. Stress includes physical factors such as hurrying to catch a bus, psychological factors such as concern over failing memory, or social factors such as retirement or moving from the familiar home and neighborhood. Obviously physical, psychological, and social factors always interact in human behavior and, in reality, the impact of each cannot be separated from that of the others.

Not only may the older person have a less than adequate reserve capacity available to handle stress effectively, but when homeostasis is disturbed in some system of an older person, a return to equilibrium is much slower than in younger persons. In summary, homeostatic equilibrium is more easily disrupted in older age by stressful situations, and once disrupted, dynamic equilibrium is more difficult to regain.

Those who work with older persons should be aware of the loss of reserve capacity in the various organ systems of the body and the resulting implications for maintaining homeostasis. Environmental manipulation and regulation of life style to reduce stress in all of its various forms have definite significant coping and adaptive value for all age groups, but are especially vital for older people who must deal with a variety of cumulating losses.

BIBLIOGRAPHY

Judge, T.G. The milieu interieur and aging. In Brocklehurst, J.C., ed., *Textbook of Geriatric Medicine and Gerontology.* Edinburgh and London: Churchill Livingstone, 1973.

Macey, Robert I. *Human Physiology,* 2nd ed. Englewood Cliffs, N.J.: Prentice-Hall, 1973.

Shock, Nathan. System integration. In Finch, Caleb E. and Hayflick, Leonard, eds., *Handbook of the Biology of Aging.* New York: Van Nostrand Reinhold, 1977.

Timiras, P.S., ed., *Developmental Physiology and Aging.* New York: Macmillan, 1972.

Unit 14

Nutrition

Health, vigor, and quality of life in childhood, adulthood, middle age, and old age depend upon adequate nutrition. Monet (24) states: "Man's future depends on what he eats." The human body needs certain basic nutrients such as carbohydrates, fats, proteins, vitamins, and water to build and repair tissues, to supply energy, and to regulate vital body processes.

The nutritional needs of the elderly are essentially the same as for others, although calorie requirements vary for each person. Physiological, psychological, and social factors alter the nutritional habits of the older population. For instance, forced modifications in family structure such as the loss of a spouse or minimal contact with family and friends produce loneliness and possible depression that may result in poor appetite. Changing patterns of activity, decreased energy, and fatigue also contribute to a loss of interest in food or a lack of appetite. Disabilities such as arthritis, stroke, and heart or lung disease prevent the elderly from shopping and preparing adequate meals. Apathy resulting from mental illness, confusion, or disorientation interferes with the motivation to eat properly.

Eating is a social event usually shared and enjoyed with others, but increasingly denied to those elderly who live alone or who are institutionalized. A sense of well-being, belonging, and happiness serve to stimulate interest in shopping and in preparing foods. Poverty, fixed retirement income, and inflation, however, prevent older persons from purchasing nutritious foods, especially foods high in protein since these tend to cost more than carbohydrate-rich food. Many older people have a tendency to snack on foods with high sugar content or "empty calories" rather than on more nutritious substances. In addition, minimal knowledge of basic nutritional needs, lifelong eating habits, and ethnic food preferences increase the probability of inadequate diet. A lack of cooking facilities or refrigeration are also contributing factors in poor nutrition.

Water is vital to human life. One-and-a-half to two quarts are needed each day to maintain stable body temperature and efficient cell metabolism, as well as to give form and structure to the body. Homeostatic mechanisms regulate fluid supply, and amounts taken in and excreted should be equal. Fluids are excreted through the lungs, skin, kidneys, and intestines. Dehydration because of too little fluid taken into the body is common in older persons and affects homeostasis adversely as well as disrupting function in major body organs such as those of the circulatory and urinary systems.

The state of the digestive system plays an important part in nutrition. Loss of teeth, improperly fitting dentures, decrease in saliva production, and reduction in the senses of taste and smell all add to a lessened interest in eating. The production of stomach enzymes and digestive juices needed for adequate digestion decreases with age and intestinal motility slows. These factors, plus lack of exercise and low intake of fluids and high bulk foods, contribute substantially to digestive problems in older people. Alcoholism, prevalent in this age group, also results in malnutrition.

Obesity is an ever-present risk factor in the aged. One survey indicates that 84 percent of men and 71 percent of women over 50 are overweight. Since food may compensate for other losses, overeating can become a substitute for the loss of employment, spouse, family, and friends. It can also be a way of achieving personal satisfaction and enjoyment.

COMMON NUTRITIONAL DEFICIENCIES

Older persons are particularly susceptible to certain basic nutritional deficiencies such as a) deficiency of vitamin D, found in sunlight or in vitamin D irradiated milk; b) deficiency of vitamin A, important for vision as well as for the condition of skin and mucous membranes; c) deficiency of vitamin C, necessary for healing, prevention of bruising, healthy gums, blood vessels, and connective tissue. Both vitamins A and C act as preventatives against infection.

Protein is necessary for the growth and maintenance of body tissue as well as for other physiologic and metabolic activities. Unfortunately, the high cost of meats, fish, and cheese contributes to this deficiency; however, lower cost foods such as beans, eggs, peas, milk, soybeans, and whole grain cereals can also supply protein requirements.

Elderly persons are more likely to become anemic because of reduced hydrochloric acid and loss of intrinsic factor (a protein) in the stomach leading to poor iron and vitamin B_{12} absorption respectively. Foods rich in iron and vitamin B_{12} such as liver, fortified cereals, and red meats should be included in every diet. In addition, anemia may be caused specifically by reduced meat intake, especially likely in older people.

Some professionals think that blood calcium levels are chronically low in most of the older members of our society due to insufficient calcium ingestion over a lifetime. Foods rich in calcium should be included in the daily diet, and some even recommend that adults take one or more grams of calcium gluconate daily. Osteoporosis, characterized by porous bones, is seen more often in postmenopausal women and is thought to be related to inadequate calcium in the diet.

Frozen foods, an unknown commodity some decades ago, are readily available food sources and have the advantage of being easy to prepare and available in small amounts. TV dinners offer a variety of basic foods at relatively low cost; however, most frozen foods are not as nutritious as fresh foods and they contain many preservatives.

DIETS FOR THE ELDERLY

About 4 or 5 percent of the population over 65 are institutionalized and require individualized health care and special diets. Many states insist that a consulting dietitian and trained dietary aides plan and prepare food served to institutional populations. Since food is extremely important to most elderly people, efforts ought to be directed towards designing more workable diet plans to include opportunities for food selection and/or a five-meal-a-day regimen. The quality of food served in institutional settings is highly variable—some facilities serve meals that are nutritious and tasty while meals at others definitely need substantial improvement.

Nutrition plays a key role in maintaining good health and facilitates recovery from illness. Modified diets are sometimes required for elderly persons with chronic disease. For instance, diabetes, most prevalent in persons over 40, calls for a reduced carbohydrate or a strict diabetic diet. Elderly individuals with heart or vascular disease often need a low sodium or low cholesterol diet. Certain drugs such as diuretics and antidepressants also make it necessary to modify the diet. It is often very difficult for elderly persons who have well-established eating habits and definite food preferences to change their dietary habits. Adopting a positive approach to nutrition in conjunction with ongoing dietary instruction, good rapport between instructor and learner, and the inclusion of favorite foods whenever possible, all help to make these adjustments easier.

Basic Foods

Basic nutrition is obtained from five sources:

1. *Meat and meat products:* Beef, veal, lamb, pork, fish, poultry, liver, and eggs. Alternates: Dry peas, beans, nuts, and peanut butter. Iron, fat, and thiamine are available from these foods. Daily requirement: two or more servings.

2. *Dairy products:* Milk, ice cream, cheese, yogurt, and butter made from skim, whole, dried, or evaporated milk. These supply calcium, protein, riboflavin, and fat. Daily requirement: two or more cups.

3. *Vegetables and fruits:* Include a deep yellow or dark green vegetable or a fruit rich in vitamin A every other day. Excellent sources are tomatoes, green leafy vegetables, peaches, apricots, bananas, watermelon, carrots, cantelope, asparagus, spinach, and squash. Citrus fruit and fruits or vegetables rich in vitamin C should be included daily. (Examples are oranges, grapefruit, tomatoes, apples, bananas, peaches, pears, strawberries, and greens.) These supply vitamins and minerals.

4. *Breads and cereals:* Whole grain, enriched or restored breads, cereals, noodles, biscuits, or rice. These supply thiamine, riboflavin, niacin, iron, and protein. Daily requirement: four or more servings a day.

5. *Fluids:* Water, juices, cocoa, coffee, tea, or other liquids. Daily requirement: one-and-a-half to two quarts a day.

Adequate nutrition in the elderly differs little from that for other adults; nevertheless, there are some basic principles that relate specifically to improved nutrition in older age. These are:

1. Fewer calories are needed because of the older person's reduced metabolism and lower levels of physical activity.

2. Reduce fat intake to 20 to 25 percent of the total calories consumed.

3. Daily protein consumption should total 1.5 to 2 grams per kilogram of body weight. Protein ought to make up 20 to 25 percent of the total caloric intake and be about equal to the intake of a healthy young adult.

4. Carbohydrate consumption should be sufficient to provide the remainder of the needed calories.

5. Adequate vitamins and minerals must be part of the daily diet, especially vitamins B and C complex, calcium, and iron.

6. Fluid amounts must be enough to result in a urine output of about 1,500 ml or one-and-a-half quarts per day. At least

six or seven glasses of fluid a day are recommended.

7. Foods such as fruits and vegetables that provide roughage in the diet are important. The prevention of constipation is dependent both upon the ingestion of roughage and on adequate amounts of water in the system.

8. Physical activity is desirable to increase the appetite and prevent constipation.

9. Eating in moderation is a must to prevent or decrease obesity.

10. Smaller, more frequent meals are helpful to eliminate snacking and they also serve as a source of greater satisfaction for some individuals.

11. If dietary habits need to be altered by introducing a special diet, a gradual transition is best, if possible, as lifelong habits are difficult to change suddenly.

12. Increased education about dietary needs is essential.

13. Salt intake should be moderate or decreased.

14. Diet planning should be personalized by taking into account individual preferences, specific nutritional needs, and idiosyncratic tolerances to various foods.

COMMUNITY BASED NUTRITION PROGRAMS

In the past several years a variety of programs aimed at promoting improved nutrition in the elderly at minimum cost have been developed. Portable meals planned by dietitians (including regular and special diets) have become available in most parts of the country. Volunteers usually deliver the food to the home and thus are able to visit with the homebound recipient. Congregate dining is also available in many areas, and various facilities, including churches, schools, and social halls now function as centers where food is prepared and served. Eating and socializing with others while participating in various recreational and educational programs meet many of the multiple needs of elderly persons. The same programs and benefits are also available at elderly day care centers.

Homemaker services are aimed at helping in the preparation of nutritious meals and assisting with light housework. These programs have been instrumental in keeping many elderly in their homes and out of institutions. Homemakers are trained in meal preparation and diet modification; in addition, a dietitian or nutritionist is available for consultation whenever needed. Another alternative is home health care in which nutritional guidance and counseling is made available and aides are employed for shopping and preparing meals.

BIBLIOGRAPHY

Books

Berger, Ruth. Nutritional needs of the aged. In Burnside, Irene M., ed., *Nursing and the Aged.* New York: McGraw-Hill, 1976.

Diekelman, Nancy. *Primary Health Care of the Well Adult.* New York: McGraw-Hill, 1977.

Hodkinson, H.M. *An Outline of Geriatrics.* New York: Academic Press, 1975.

Marble, Beulah and Patterson, Isabel. Nutrition and aging. In Spencer, Marian G. and Dorr, Caroline J., eds., *Understanding Aging: A Multidisciplinary Approach.* New York: Appleton-Century-Crofts, 1975.

Schroeder, Henry. Nutrition. In Steinberg, Franz U., ed., *Cowdry's the Care of the Geriatric Patient.* 5th ed., St. Louis: Mosby, 1976.

Periodicals

Caird, F.I., Judge, T.G., and Mcleod, C. Pointers to possible malnutrition in the elderly at home. *Gerontologica Clinica 17:*47, 1975.

Dreizen, S. Clinical manifestations of malnutrition. *Geriatrics 29:*97, 1974.

Eddy, T.P. Nutritional needs of the old. *Nursing Times 70:*1499, 1974.

Howell, Sandra and Loeb, M.B. Nutrition and Aging. *Gerontologist 9:*entire issue, 1969, pt. II.

Krehl, W.A. The influence of nutritional environment on aging. *Geriatrics 29:*65, 1974.

Langan, M.J. and Yearick, E.S. The effects of improved oral hygiene on taste perception and nutrition of the elderly. *Journal of Gerontology 31:*413, 1976.

Mayer, J. Aging and nutrition. *Geriatrics 29:*57, 1974.

Morgan, Agnes F. Nutrition of the aging. *Gerontologist 2:*77, 1962.

Sherwood, S. Sociology of food and eating: implications for action for the elderly. *American Journal of Clinical Nutrition 26:*1108, 1973.

Winick, Myron. Nutrition and aging. *Contemporary Nutrition 2:*1, 1977.

Young, C.M. Nutritional counseling for better health. *Geriatrics 29:*83, 1974.

Unit 15

Exercise

Although we do not know how to stop the aging process, there is increasing evidence that regular systematic exercise and proper nutrition enhance quality of life throughout the entire life span.

This evidence suggests that many of the aches and pains commonly associated with older age in our mechanized and sedentary society result more from poor nutritional habits and lack of physical fitness than from the aging process per se. Exercise and fitness programs for older persons are still relatively new areas of interest in this coutry, but so far results are promising and optimistic.

Herbert deVries (25) has been one of the most systematic researchers in fitness conditioning for older persons. In his studies older subjects were found to respond very well to fitness training and were able to improve their physical condition more than had been expected. Positive changes occurred, particularly in the cardiovascular system, respiratory system, muscular system, and body form (less fat and better muscle tone).

Lawrence Frankel and colleagues (26, 27) have evolved a program concerned with primary prevention (habilitation) called Project Preventicare to encourage the development and maintenance of fitness in the older population. They are convinced that regular planned exercise slows many behavior-limiting changes that are bothersome to older persons, especially muscular aches and pains, chronic fatigue, and poor circulation.

Types of exercises most suitable to older age groups are usually those which maximize rhythmic activity of large muscle masses. Walking is one of the best, but jogging, running, bicycling, swimming, and properly designed calisthenics are also very effective and enjoyable. Some form of exercise is not only appropriate but necessary for virtually everyone, as exercise can and should be individualized and tailored to take each person's own health status and body condition into consideration. Most fitness experts recommend that those over 30 have a medical examination before embarking on a systematic physical fitness program of any sort. Exercise programs should be gradual and progress made over time rather than too quickly by engaging in long, intensive, strenuous sessions; above all, exercise must be regular and habitual, and it should be fun. Fitness is more difficult to maintain as one grows older, so regular systematic exercise is a must. Exercising at least four or five times a week is desirable and often necessary to maintain good fitness levels.

Some of the numerous reported benefits of exercise and proper diet for older persons are increased muscle strength, better coordination, greater stamina and body flexibility, less fatigue, fewer digestive problems and less constipation, improved sleep, reduced back pain, and less joint stiffness. Perhaps a more important gain is an increase in cardiovascular and respiratory efficiency allowing more oxygen to be delivered to body cells for increasingly efficient metabolism and body functioning. One of the most enjoyable benefits of physical fitness is a hard-to-define, but invigorating-to-experience enhanced sense of well-being.

It is unfortunate that part of our cultural folklore seems to encourage inactivity with age. "Sit down and take it easy; you've earned a rest" is poor advice at any age, but it is especially detrimental for middle- and older-aged persons. The long-lived cultures studied by Leaf (28) in which people live to be 100 and beyond are all characterized by a lifetime of continuous physical activity. Other variables such as genetic influence, climate, diet, lack of tension or stress, and meaningful social roles all appear to contribute to such longevity, but physical activity is certainly one vital and consistent factor.

The best advice for reducing many of the woes of growing old seems to be "use it or lose it," and it's easier to use it and not lose it than to lose it and try to regain it. A number of beneficial exercise programs for older persons are available, ranging from calisthenics to yoga.

BIBLIOGRAPHY

Books

Christensen, Alice and Rankin, David. *"Easy Does It" Yoga for People Over Sixty*. Cleveland: Saraswati Studios, Inc., 1975.

deVries, Herbert A. *Vigor Regained*. Englewood Cliffs, N.J.: Prentice-Hall, 1974.

Harris, Raymond and Frankel, Lawrence J., eds. *Guide to Fitness After Fifty*. New York: Plenum, 1977.

The National Association for Human Development, *Join the Active People Over Sixty!* The National Association for Human Development, P.O. Box 100, Washington, D.C. 20044.

Simri, Uriel, ed. *Physical Exercise and Activity for the Aging*. Center for the Study of Aging, 706 Madison Ave., New York, N.Y. 12208.

Unit 16

Organic Brain Syndrome

Organic brain syndrome (OBS) is a neuropsychiatric disorder caused by or related to impairment in brain cell functioning. A variety of psychiatric symptoms may be associated with organic brain syndrome; however, the same psychiatric symptoms may also show themselves in a person who does not have organic brain damage.

The presenting symptoms alone are not sufficient justification for the label of organic brain syndrome. To further complicate understanding, diagnostic classifications and terminology have not been used consistently or precisely over the years. The interested reader should refer to references at the end of this chapter for some of the newer sources of information.

Organic brain syndrome is differentiated into a) *acute or reversible brain syndrome;* and b) *chronic or irreversible brain syndrome.* The two types sometimes occur together or each may occur with various other types of mental illness. Symptoms appear suddenly or slowly over a long period of time. The classic symptoms associated with organic brain syndrome are a) disorientation for time, place, and person; b) memory loss; c) disturbances in thinking, especially in abstract thinking and reasoning; d) impairment of judgment; and e) emotional lability, or inappropriate emotional responses. Some or all of these symptoms may be present in a person. The degree of severity ranges from mild to moderate to severe and is an important determinant of whether an individual can remain independent or must be institutionalized. Diagnosis is extremely difficult as several physiological and psychological conditions may exist in an individual at the same time.

All organic brain disease of later life was at one time thought to be irreversible. In fact, the lack of adequate diagnosis has been one reason for the delayed development and application of therapeutic techniques to very old people. Such interest is still very new in gerontology and geriatrics.

ACUTE BRAIN SYNDROME

Acute brain syndrome, or reversible brain syndrome, has also been referred to in the past as senile delusional state and senile delirium. Pfeiffer (29) estimates that 10 to 20 percent of the elderly have reversible OBS. Causes include such factors as drug intoxication, metabolic disorders, malnutrition, congestive heart failure, and many other conditions which tax the person's reserve capacity or ability to cope. Acute brain disorders are potentially reversible once the cause has been determined and remedial action taken.

CHRONIC BRAIN SYNDROME

Chronic brain syndrome (CBS) or irreversible brain syndrome is also referred to as senile brain disease, senile dementia, or senility. Three types of CBS may be differentiated:

Senile Psychosis.   Senile psychosis is related to diffuse brain cell loss, especially in the cerebral cortex. The cause is unknown. The only clear correlation between the amount of cell loss and observable behavior changes seems to be that those with the largest cell loss are likely to show the most symptoms. *Where* cell loss occurs in the brain is essentially just as important as the amount of loss. In addition to the actual amount and location of cell loss, such factors as the rapidity of cell loss, basic personality, and type of living environment have a definite impact on overt behavior. Integrated, adjusted personalities seem to handle these organic changes more successfully than others, and those in a supportive environment function more effectively than those in an environment which is too challenging, or not challenging enough.

Symptoms of senile psychosis include short- and long-term memory impairment, visual-motor coordination difficulties, inability to understand abstract concepts, lack of flexibility in problem-solving and in learning new information, and disorientation to one's environment. Such symptoms are not associated exclusively with senile psychosis, however, and a thorough diagnostic assessment is necessary for an accurate evaluation.

Arteriosclerotic Psychosis. Psychosis due to arteriosclerotic brain disease is another form of CBS. Caused by loss of brain cells from lack of oxygen and necessary nutrients, it is at times difficult to distinguish from senile psychosis. Usually arteriosclerotic brain disease progresses more erratically than the steady deterioration associated with senile psychosis, but if a series of small brain areas with restricted blood flow die, behavior associated with the accumulated cell loss may easily parrot that of senile psychosis.

Presenile Dementia. Two of the most common forms of presenile dementia are *Alzheimer's disease* and *Pick's disease.* In both, symptoms appear in the late 40s or 50s and decline is usually rapid. Characteristic behavior changes are deterioration of intellectual skills and disorganization of personality.

SUMMARY

In working with older people it is imperative not to classify each bit of idiosyncratic behavior as senility (organic brain syndrome). Senility is an inaccurate, misunderstood, over-used term and has been responsible for much unfair stereotyping of old age behavior. For example, if a person shows memory loss (such as inability to remember a telephone number) at age 45, that's all right, but if the same behavior appears at 75, it's suspect and likely to be interpreted as impending "senility."

Senility has for too long implied irreversible and inevitable consequences of growing older. We now recognize that not all older people become senile, while some individuals are excellent examples of senility at age 40. We also now know that senility in some instances is reversible; if not reversible, behavior can often be modified in very old people if they are motivated to want to change. Newer treatment techniques such as reality orientation, remotivation, sensory retraining, life review therapy, and others are encouraging and useful even with many who have moderate to severe organic brain damage. An excellent summary of these techniques has been prepared by Barns, Sack, and Shore. (30)

Older people have shown themselves to be appropriate candidates for various forms of psychotherapy and many of them demonstrate marked improvement in behaviors heretofore considered to be "just an inevitable part of growing old." Muriel Oberleder (31) suggests that senility is a form of psychosis or mental breakdown in the elderly and should be treated as such. She states that anxiety produces senile symptoms and that there are more situations that create anxiety in older age as losses accumulate, while at the same time there are usually fewer opportunities to reduce anxiety. Such situations could easily produce emotional breakdown. Putting the "problems of old age" into perspective as problems of individuals with different personalities, varied past experiences, and unique biological systems, instead of writing them off as the inevitabilities of old age, is a step in the right direction. The use of positive rehabilitative and therapeutic techniques with older people is a new, challenging, exciting, and optimistic area of endeavor.

BIBLIOGRAPHY
Books

Burnside, Irene M. Acute and chronic brain syndrome. In Burnside, Irene M., ed., *Nursing and the Aged.* New York: McGraw-Hill, 1976.
Butler, Robert N. and Lewis, Myrna I. *Aging and Mental Health,* 2nd ed. St. Louis: Mosby, 1977.
Taulbee, Lucille. Reality orientation and the aged. In Burnside, Irene M., ed., *Nursing and the Aged.* op. cit.
Verwoerdt, Adrian. *Clinical Geropsychiatry.* Baltimore: Williams and Wilkins, 1976.

Periodicals

Libow, Leslie S. Pseudo-senility: acute and reversible organic brain syndromes. *Journal of the American Geriatrics Society 21:*112, 1973.
Reichel, W. Organic brain syndromes in the aged. *Hospital Practitioner 11:*119, 1976.
Wells, C.E. Dementia reconsidered. *Archives of General Psychiatry 26:*385, 1972.

Unit 17

Drugs

Multiple chronic health problems develop as we age. In an attempt to prevent or treat chronic disease many elderly look upon the hundreds of drugs available today as curative or at least life prolonging. Twenty-five percent of all prescription drugs are consumed by elders, who spend three times the amount of money on drugs than do the other age groups.

Along with drugs prescribed by physicians, over-the-counter drugs are taken for ailments such as headaches, colds, or constipation. Is it any wonder, then, that many persons with multiple illnesses consume at least four to eight different pills daily, and possibly as many as 12 to 20 or more?

Medications are not without their dangers. It is estimated that 15 to 30 percent of those hospitalized give evidence of one or more reactions to drugs. It has been stated that drug side effects are responsible for 30,000 deaths and 1.5 million admissions to hospitals each year. Older persons are more prone to experience toxic effects from drugs they ingest than younger persons; therefore, any unusual symptom caused by a drug should be reported to a physician immediately and the drug should be discontinued until clarification is obtained.

The action of drugs in the body is directly related to the processes of absorption, distribution, metabolism, and excretion, all of which become less efficient in the aging individual. Absorption is altered by age-related changes in the gastrointestinal system, and the distribution of drugs depends upon effective heart functioning and circulation. Actually, the overall decreased efficiency of the cardiovascular system affects the rate of distribution, metabolism, and excretion of drugs.

Age-related changes in the liver and kidney disturb the rate of metabolism and excretion so that drugs are retained in the body longer. Dosages of drugs should be prescribed on the basis of the time it takes for half the dose to be eliminated from the body, as drugs often remain in the body for prolonged periods, causing drug accumulation and toxic effects.

It is imperative that drugs be prescribed on an individual basis, that the fewest possible be prescribed, and that priority be given to the most important diseases. Preferably, the smallest amount of a drug that will have a therapeutic effect should be administered initially. The dosage can then be increased gradually if necessary. A periodic review of the drug regimen by a physician is necessary to prevent the total number of prescription and nonprescription drugs from increasing to unnecessary numbers.

Some commonly prescribed medications are known to have negative effects upon the older person's body. Multiple drugs taken concurrently sometimes interact with one another or with certain foods or alcohol causing toxic symptoms. We shall, therefore, review some of the more frequently used drugs and their side effects and interactions.

DRUGS FOR HEART DISEASE

The incidence of heart disease is high among elders and some form of digitalis is often used to strengthen and slow the heartbeat. Symptoms of digitalis toxicity include irregular heartbeat, nausea, vomiting, blurred vision, headache, confusion, and psychosis. Other drugs, such as Butazolidin prescribed for arthritis, and Orinase for diabetes, may enhance the effects of digitalis. Conversely, the effectiveness of digitalis may be decreased by phenobarbital and other sedatives.

Diuretics (water pills) taken to rid the body of excess fluid cause dehydration and an imbalance in important body chemicals such as sodium and potassium. Harmful interactions of digitalis and diuretics deplete the body of these chemicals, causing serious side effects. Persons using these drugs need potassium supplied by fresh fruit (such as bananas or oranges) or potassium supplements. Diuretics interact with Orinase to elevate the blood sugar. For individuals who have gout these drugs may also elevate the uric acid levels.

Cardiovascular diseases prompt the use of reserpine to lower the blood pressure. This drug produces depression in the elderly, many of whom are already depressed. Since depression develops slowly and sometimes includes agitation and suicidal tendencies, special observation of the individual taking this medication is necessary.

DRUGS FOR ARTHRITIS

Aspirin, a popular drug sold over the counter, is often used to control arthritic pains and other ailments of the aging. Side effects, which are experienced more often by older persons, include ringing in the ears, stomach irritation, bleeding, rashes, nausea, vomiting, confusion, and deafness. Among the drugs it interacts with are anticoagulants, whose action it enhances, causing bleeding and even more serious conditions such as strokes. The oral drugs used for diabetes may also be potentiated by aspirin.

Several medications are prescribed for arthritis. These include:

1. Butazolidin, responsible for numerous side effects that may be fatal to those in the older age group. It should be used sparingly, for a short period of time, and with close attention by a physician.

2. Corticosteroids, noted for their many serious reactions such as gastric distress or ulcers, personality problems, depression, and even psychosis.

3. Indocin, responsible for gastrointestinal distress, eye changes, mental disorders, and parkinsonism.

From this list it can readily be seen that persons with arthritis should be knowledgeable about the drugs they are taking and their possible side effects.

ANTIDEPRESSANTS

Antidepressants and tranquilizers are among the top ten of the most frequently prescribed drugs. For the elderly, however, doses should begin at half the adult dose and increase slowly since side effects are numerous and include disturbed equilibrium, drowsiness, reduced blood pressure, delirium agitation, and parkinsonism. Drug accumulation in the body is common and can result in motor disturbances that predispose the person to falls and fractures. Taken concurrently with alcohol, many of these drugs can have serious or fatal effects. Antidepressants and tranquilizers are used all too frequently to keep the elderly "less agitated and more manageable." Rehabilitative programs, improved nursing care, and more individual attention could drastically reduce drug use and result in more alert and "in tune with the world" older persons.

DRUGS FOR DIABETES

Diabetes, a chronic illness prevalent among persons over 45 is usually observed in a less severe form among the elderly than in the young. This disease is controlled by insulin injections, oral hypoglycemic pills, and/or diet. Since diabetes is often mild in this age group, many individuals are able to regulate the disease by pills or diet. Both insulin and the oral medication need to be carefully monitored, though, as low blood sugar may result. Side effects of hypoglycemic pills include jaundice, sensitivity to light, and alcohol intolerance.

HYPNOTICS

Sleeping patterns in old age change so that sleep is not as deep and awakenings are more frequent. Hypnotics (sleeping pills) prescribed by a physician or purchased over the counter are often used to promote sleep. These are frequently abused by the elderly and health caregivers. Other means, such as a glass of warm milk, a back rub, or sincere concern by others, might accomplish better results. Side effects of hypnotics include confusion, ataxia (uncoordinated movements), gastric irritation, excessive drowsiness during the day, and severe "hangover" at night. Some sleeping pills contain scopolamine and should be used with caution by persons who have glaucoma. Drug reactions may affect cognitive functioning during the day and are likely to account for the stuporous behavior often observed in nursing home or hospital patients.

LAXATIVES

After viewing television and reading the many ads for laxatives it might seem that the elderly cannot function without them. This seems to be the case with many who take them in abundance. Instead of exercising daily, eating properly (especially roughage foods), and drinking adequate amounts of fluid, laxatives are taken, causing dependency, dehydration, loss of muscle tone in the intestines, loss of important salts and minerals, and reduced absorption of vitamins A and D. If laxatives are needed regularly for constipation, a physician should be consulted. Keep in mind that some drugs taken by the elderly for other ailments also cause constipation. Drugs are not the answer to every health problem experienced by older persons. Changes in life style, physical exercise, mental stimulation, and social interaction may "work miracles."

ATTITUDES TOWARD "PILL-POPPING"

Quackery is an ever present threat to proper medication regimens. Special medicines, treatments, and cures appear on the market from time to time promising to cure common ailments of the elderly. Not only are these expensive, but they may cause the person to delay medical treatment, which could prove fatal.

Attitudes toward the ingestion of medications are highly varied among the aged. Some believe that all medication is worthless and, following a visit to the physician, do not take the prescribed medications. Others will use pills when critically ill but discard them as soon as improvement is noted. Still others hold fixed, inaccurate ideas about what a particular pill will do to them. Some older people indulge in overmedication, and pills, cough medicines, laxatives, and so on, both physician and self-prescribed, fill their medicine cabinets and accumulate over years.   Bertram Moss writes that patients often arrive at nursing homes with bags of medications (32). He evaluated the number and kinds of drugs his patients really needed, calling this evaluation a "drying out" process. His findings revealed that many were suffering from the side effects of overmedication rather than from too little medication.   Richard Henry (33) described a similar "drying out" experience in a health care setting as "much like Easter Sunday morning in every room." As the number of drugs was cut in half, the patients were resurrected from their beds and chairs and the number of ambulatory patient days doubled. Many of the elderly are overly dependent upon drugs and some are indeed addicted.

PREVENTION OF DRUG ACCIDENTS

Lack of accurate information about drugs is common in the older age group. Some believe that if one pill helps, two will be sure to cure. Medications are forgotten or confused, especially if several have been prescribed. After the first bottle of medicine has been taken the prescription may not be refilled due to misunderstanding or because of a lack of money. Another example of drug abuse is swapping pills with friends, a common but dangerous practice.

Inaccurate information about how and when drugs are to be taken can be serious. When five or six pills are prescribed for different times during the day, even a young person has difficulty remembering when to take what. Placing the medicines in small glasses and labeling them can prevent confusion. Writing down the various types of pills and times to be taken on the calendar or making lists that name and describe them is helpful. Setting the alarm clock to ring when medications are due can be an especially useful reminder for the forgetful or slightly confused person. Having medications monitored by a relative or friend can also be of value. Pill containers that have seven compartments, one for each day of the week, also encourage a proper drug regimen. Physicians and pharmacists should clearly identify each medication, what it is for, and the directions for its use on the outside of each bottle. The elderly themselves ought to ask questions when in doubt.

Safety caps on medicine bottles have proven to be a real challenge for all ages, but other types of caps can be requested when prescriptions are filled. Professionals have a responsibility to teach the older person facts about the disease the drug is used for, the name of the medication, what its action is, its side effects, times it is to be taken, how it is to be taken, and the foods, drinks, or other medications to avoid while using it. This information should be in writing and checked repeatedly to make sure the person understands it. All too often the elderly, especially those with sensory losses, are misinformed or do not understand, and it is not until a drug reaction or serious illness results that the consequences of misunderstanding are appreciated.

SUMMARY

Medications are of tremendous value to many of the elderly whose very lives may depend upon the continued ingestion of various prescribed drugs. Nevertheless, knowledge and understanding of age-related factors that influence absorption, distribution, metabolism, and excretion of these drugs is imperative for reaction-free treatment. To ensure optimal physical, psychological, and social well-being, drug dosages should be as low as possible, the number of drugs taken should be minimal, and an evaluation of their effectiveness should be made on a regular basis. With such a treatment plan, drugs will prevent disease, permit comfortable living, and even cure many existing illnesses.

BIBLIOGRAPHY

Books

Butler, Robert and Lewis, Myrna. *Aging and Mental Health,* 2nd ed. St. Louis: Mosby, 1977.

Conahan, Judith. *Helping Your Elderly Patients: A Guide for Nursing Assistants.* New York: Tiresias Press, 1976.

Davis, Richard H., ed. *Drugs and the Elderly.* Los Angeles: University of Southern California Press, 1975.

Hodkinson, H.M. *An Outline of Geriatrics.* New York: Academic Press, 1975.

Kayne, Ronald. Drugs and the elderly. In Burnside, Irene M., ed., *Nursing and the Aged.* New York: McGraw-Hill, 1976.

Shafer, Kathleen; Sawyer, Janet; McClusky, Audrey; Beck, Edna and Phipps, Wilma. *Medical Surgical Nursing.* St. Louis: Mosby, 1975.

Periodicals

Anderson, W.F. Administration, labelling, and general principles of drug prescription in the elderly. *Gerontologica Clinica 16:*4, 1974.

Benson, R.A. and Brodie, D.C. Suicide by overdoses of medicines among the aged. *Journal of the American Geriatrics Society 23:*304, 1975.

Berman, P.M. and Kirsner, J.B. Recognizing and avoiding adverse gastro-intestinal effects of drugs. *Geriatrics 29:*59, 1974.

Davidson, J.R. Trail of self-medication in the elderly. *Nursing Times 70:*391, 1974.

Davison, W. Factors complicating the effectiveness of drugs. *Gerontologica Clinica 16:*64, 1974.

Eisdorfer, Carl. Observations on the psychopharmacology of the aged. *Journal of the American Geriatrics Society 23:*53, 1975.

Freeman, J.T. Some principles of medication in geriatrics. *Journal of the American Geriatrics Society 22:*289, 1974.

Hall, M.R.P. Adverse drug reaction in the elderly. *Gerontologica Clinica 16:*175, 1974.

Hodkinson, H.M. Biochemical side effects of drugs in the elderly. *Gerontologica Clinica 16:*175, 1974.

MacLennan, W.J. Drug interactions. *Gerontologica Clinica 16:*18, 1974.

Means, B.J. and Lamy, P.P. Diagnostic tests, drugs, and the geriatric patient. *Journal of the American Geriatrics Society 22:*258, 1974.

Pascarelli, E.F. Drug dependence: an age-old problem compounded by old age. *Geriatrics 29:*109, 1974.

Shields, Eldonna M. Introduction to drug therapy for older adults. *Journal of Gerontological Nursing 1:*8, 1975.

Unit 18

Teaching the Older Adult

As the population increases to include greater numbers of people over age 65, the need for teaching techniques appropriate for older adults becomes more imperative. Learning is a lifelong process that should begin in infancy and end only when it becomes physically and mentally impossible to learn.

Educators must take into consideration that over this broad span of years both the needs of the learner and his/her learning abilities may change. In the past, methods of teaching children have received top priority in education, but as learning is now becoming more a part of every person's life throughout the life span, methods of teaching older adults are justifiably receiving significantly more attention.

Older adults have a wide variety of interests and needs and are consequently participating in diverse types of learning situations. Enrollment at colleges, universities, and adult education classes is on the increase. In addition, numerous specialized seminars and short courses on such topics as social security, protecting self or home, investment planning, cooking, crafts, and other practical subjects are attended by large numbers of elderly persons. There is increased demand for such essential information as health education involving disease prevention, knowledge of special diets or medications, and the management of such medical problems as, for example, diabetes or a fractured hip.

Older persons experience cumulating losses that may have a great impact on physical, social, and psychological areas of life.

It is extremely important, then, for teachers of older persons to be acutely aware of how such losses affect the learning process as well as what methods can be used to facilitate the learning process.

FACTORS THAT INFLUENCE LEARNING IN THE OLDER ADULT

Physical Factors

Some physical changes associated with age affect the older adult's ability to learn as quickly or as well as a younger person. Certain changes occurring in the musculoskeletal and nervous systems result in slower psychomotor reactions so that performing new skills may be physically difficult. Additional time, therefore, is often needed for the older adult to complete certain learning tasks. Specific health problems such as arthritis, Parkinson's disease, fractures, and generalized decreased energy and stamina make sitting for long periods of time difficult and uncomfortable. Persons with organic brain disease and arteriosclerosis obviously find it hard to learn new intellectual and psychomotor tasks.

Changes in Vision. Sharpness or acuity of vision decreases with age as does accommodation—the ability to focus on objects at different distances. Pupil size decreases, the lens becomes less transparent and more yellow, and cataracts are common. The colors orange, red, and yellow are more easily perceived in older age than are blues, greens, and purples.

Changes in Audition. Hearing is also often impaired as a function of age, especially the ability to hear conversation as opposed to pure tone sounds. Sometimes speech sounds cannot be easily distinguished from other sounds, making normal conversation more difficult to follow accurately.

Changes in the Senses of Taste, Touch, and Smell. All of these special sensory systems change with age and gradually become less efficient, although there is substantial variation between individuals in the amount of loss. These particular age-related changes, however, do not seem to interfere appreciably with ability to learn as do changes in vision and hearing.

Psychological Factors

Psychological changes associated with age are also extremely important in learning. The ability to learn actually shows little decrease with age, but motivation, physical disease, attitude, perception, and attention are among the many factors influencing learning, especially in the older adult. Continued lifelong mental stimulation and interest in new ideas facilitate learning; lack of confidence in one's ability to learn, not uncommon in members of older age groups, may be the greatest hindrance.

Changes in Ability to Learn. Certain psychological changes may occur with age and interfere with efficient learning. For example, the older learner tends to solve problems by using methods he/she already knows and is less likely than younger learners to use new information or new methods. Such inflexible problem solving orientations are least obvious in those with the most formal education, those with higher intelligence, and those who have participated over the years in educational endeavors.

Although standard intelligence tests indicate that measured IQ declines with age (especially as measured by speed of response and ability to integrate abstract information), verbal abilities and information accrued over the years usually remain intact or increase with age. Aging individuals are characteristically slower in receiving information through sensory receptors, slower in processing it in the nervous system, and slower in acting upon incoming information, but the majority are able to continue learning well into old age.

Changes in Memory. Memory, especially for recent events, decreases with age for many, but not for all. Such decreases may be due simply to lack of interest or lessened ability to concentrate on the salient aspects of a task to be learned. Memory loss may be affected by time factors in that older information has been rehearsed and used many times over the years, whereas recent information is not as well integrated. In addition, extraneous noise and distractions can also interfere with the ability to remember recent events if it is difficult for one to concentrate. Psychopathology is another possible reason for memory loss that ought not to be overlooked in assessing teaching-learning situations.

Older persons learn best when they are allowed to pace themselves rather than when they are forced into a pre-set pattern. Effective instruction should omit irrelevant information. Tasks should be simplified, instructional material should be well-organized, and provision should be made for success experiences in order to motivate the learners to increase their efforts. Being sensitive to the fears, personal concerns, and psychological status of elders is especially important in effective teaching-learning.

Sociological Factors

Various social factors influence learning in the older adult. For instance, assuming meaningful roles in society contributes to a sense of self-identity and personal worth, while retirement frequently results in role changes that decrease the individual's sense of worth and reduce his/her motivation to learn. Cultural and religious differences must also be considered in teaching, for new ideas and concepts may be rejected by the elderly without evaluation if they conflict with strong personal values and lifelong beliefs. Effective communication obviously depends upon a language level comprehensible to both teacher and learner.

TEACHING TECHNIQUES

Providing a Setting for Learning

The physical learning environment can either facilitate or inhibit learning. The learning process will be helped considerably if it takes place in a cheerful room with good lighting and acoustics, proper temperature control, and comfortable chairs arranged informally. Extraneous visual or auditory stimuli, though, may detract from the learning environment and should be eliminated to the extent possible. Other physical factors to consider are accessibility of the classroom, elimination of environmental barriers such as stairs, and convenient restroom facilities.

Teaching Methods

Teaching can be provided through a variety of methods.

One-to-One Instruction. The most commonly used method is one-to-one instruction in which there is much interaction between the teacher and the learner. By employing eye contact, by speaking clearly, and by showing sincere personal interest in the students, a teacher will encourage learning.

Teaching Machines. The use of teaching machines is another method of individual teaching-learning. If teaching machines are unfamiliar to the students, they may feel apprehensive about them. If this is the case, they should be taught how to use the machines correctly and should be allowed enough practice with them to become comfortable using them before actual instruction begins. Active involvement in learning and logical presentation of material are two advantages of this type of instruction. The teacher should seek feedback from students about their program and should provide positive reinforcement such as praise and social approval at frequent intervals.

Programmed Instruction. This is a third type of individual instruction and, if well constructed, has the advantage of providing carefully planned, and well-organized sequences of basic concepts to the learner slowly. In addition, it gives the student constant opportunities to check his/her individual learning progress.

Group Instruction. Group instruction is usually a highly supportive and secure situation for the adult learner. Creating a pleasant, nonthreatening atmosphere free of competition and criticism generates participation and facilitates learning. All learners should be encouraged to ask questions and then should receive appropriate positive reinforcements such as approval and praise for their participation.

Many variables contribute to successful group instruction:

1. Since many adults tend to be problem-oriented, they may respond better to concrete examples than to theoretical abstractions. Learning will be easier and more relevant if they can relate information from their own experiences and use their own particular talents as part of the learning process.

2. Overall learning goals should, ideally, be developed jointly by instructor and learner using short-term goals as achievable points along the way to the long-term goal. Genuine involvement in the learning process by both instructor and learner is crucial for maintaining ongoing interest and continued effort. Effective and organized use of teaching time promotes positive attitudes toward learning and makes the situation more relevant for the older learner.

3. Pacing the presentation of new material to meet the individual needs of learners is of utmost importance in group instruction. New concepts should be presented at a comfortable rate to permit understanding, assimilation, and application. A variety of teaching aids such as films, models, pictures, handouts, demonstrations, student reports, video-taping, filmstrips, discussions, lectures, posters, photographs, creative ex-

periences, and field trips all help to increase comprehension of subject matter. Active participation in class allows for clarification of newly learned ideas and concepts.

Since the elderly may be expected to learn somewhat more slowly than younger adults, materials should also be presented in writing and in logical, organized sequences. Small units are preferable because they are easier to assimilate than large units of new material. Several presentations of the same concept using different techniques facilitate learning, but the instructor must be careful not to oversimplify to the point of insulting the mature adult.

4. Class length and the time of meeting should be determined by the desires of the group insofar as possible. Since sitting for prolonged periods is difficult for many, one-half to one hour sessions may be preferable and can be comfortably tolerated by most. In planning, remember that many older persons prefer not to drive after dark and others may be accustomed to an afternoon rest.

5. Some participants may "take over the class." This can create a delicate situation in which feelings may be hurt and other group members may become bored. Encouraging participation by all members of the group, presenting a schedule of activities for each session, and suggesting that a talkative participant help another student may somewhat relieve the problem of domination by one member.

6. Learning is certainly more likely to take place when the older person is not preoccupied with pressing personal problems such as illness, loss of a spouse, or other special individual concerns. At times these situations must be resolved before active involvement in the learning process is possible.

TEACHING PERSONS WITH SENSORY DEFICITS

Sensory deficits in learners present a particular challenge for an instructor. Some suggested methods of improving the learning climate for sensory handicapped persons are offered here, but many others can be generated by a sensitive teacher who understands the special problems of his/her students.

Visually Handicapped Persons

If the learners have eyeglasses, they should be worn, be properly fitted, and be clean; magnifying devices may be used to augment eyeglasses. The light source should be bright, but not glaring; students should not face the light directly. When using diagrams, visual aids, or printed matter, large print with distinct figures in contrasting colors is most visible; orange, red, and yellow are most easily discriminated by older adults. Typing should always be double spaced. Sitting near the instructor or source of information is also helpful to those whose vision is severely impaired. Special recordings or tapes of books and magazines, plus large-print reading materials can be obtained in most states at little or no cost and will make learning much easier for the partially sighted or blind.

Hard of Hearing Persons

To maximize hearing ability, the speaking voice should be lowered, as well as the sounds of audiovisual materials. Eliminate extraneous noises that distract or interfere with speech perception. Speaking slowly, distinctly, and in a low tone maximizes a hearing-impaired person's ability to hear and understand. Be aware of the learner's reactions to speech that indicate he/she is not hearing well. Such reactions include leaning forward, turning the good ear, cupping the ear, or a puzzled facial expression. Ask the group if you are speaking clearly enough and try to avoid distracting gestures. Stimulating the use of several senses through visual materials, auditory messages, and the use of touch and smell is also advantageous in teaching. When questions are asked, repeat them so the entire group can hear and benefit from the question and answer exchange. The teacher should consistently try to determine if all the learners are following and understanding each presentation.

SUMMARY

Older persons should be encouraged to take advantage of learning opportunities. Too many believe that as aging progresses, learning is no longer possible. It is important, then, to design and apply specialized teaching techniques, based on an understanding of age-related system changes, to develop effective learning environments in an effort to enhance the pleasure, enjoyment, and human growth that learning offers to every human being.

BIBLIOGRAPHY

Books

Christopherson, Victor A., Coulter, Pearl P. and Wolanin, Mary O., eds. *Rehabilitation Nursing.* New York: McGraw-Hill, 1974.

Knowles, Malcolm. *The Adult Learner: A Neglected Species.* Houston: Gulf Publishing, 1972.

Long Huey B. *Are They Ever Too Old to Learn?* Englewood Cliffs, N.J.: Prentice-Hall, 1971.

Murray, Ruth and Zentner, Judith. *Nursing Concepts for Health Promotion.* Englewood Cliffs, N.J.: Prentice-Hall, 1975.

Spencer, Marion and Dorr, Caroline, eds. *Understanding Aging: A Multidisciplinary Approach.* New York: Appleton-Century-Crofts, 1975.

Periodicals

Hallburg, Jeanne C. The teaching of aged adults. *Gerontological Nursing 11:*13, 1976.

Hendrickson, Andrew. Adult learning and the adult learner. *Adult Leadership 14:*254, 1966.

Mason, W. Dean. Aging and lifelong learning. *Journal of Research and Development in Education 7:*68, 1974.

Peterson, David A. Older person's nutrition and adult education. *Adult Leadership 11:*261, 1973.

Stanford, E. Percil. Education and aging: new task for education. *Adult Leadership 20:*281, 1972.

Unit 19

Death and Dying

Each day death comes to over 5,000 Americans. It comes in many forms—suddenly while at work, slowly after an illness, during sleep or play, anywhere, any place, any time. As sure as we were born we will die, yet, as with many unpleasant thoughts, concern with death is put out of mind until gradually old age is upon us. Friends and relatives die and fewer meaningful persons are left.

How often have we heard older people say, "I'm the last one of my family and most of my friends are gone, too." Death is primarily an experience of old age, for almost two-thirds of those who die each year are over age 65 (34).

Throughout life we are faced with certain developmental tasks to be resolved. One of the tasks of older age is the acceptance of the inevitability of death. As life progresses to old age, losses begin to accumulate. Children are born, reared, then leave home; parents, relatives, and friends die; retirement implies loss of a long-time and often personally important social role; the old home may be sold in favor of a smaller living unit; and physical decrements of age and disease increase in number and intensity. Having read hundreds of interviews that nursing students have had with the elderly, it is apparent to the authors of this book that death is a topic many elders think about frequently. Nevertheless, in our society death is a mysterious event that most of us avoid thinking of or talking about. When we do speak of death we use euphemisms such as "passed away," "gone," "expired," or "resting in peace." We do not like to use the words "dead" or "died."

Since most deaths occur in hospitals or nursing homes away from family and friends, people are able to avoid the full impact of their relatives' and friends' deaths. Even after a death, denial is evident as the body is immediately removed by the mortician, who prepares and dresses it to be viewed as though it were still alive. Children may even be deprived of realistic associations with death when a pet animal dies, for they may be told that the pet ran away or that someone took it. Thus, many persons go through life shielded from death and supported in this repudiation of reality by a death-denying society. Is it any wonder, then, that death is an experience to be denied? Cicely Saunders, famous for her affiliation with St. Christopher's Hospice in England, believes that death is not so terrible if we learn throughout life that it is a part of living.

In some cultures the family constellation is preserved and older persons maintain positions of honor and dignity. In such cultures meaningful religious rituals and the constant attention of family members are important supports in dying and death that our present system of impersonal health care all but destroys. As a rule, relationships with family and friends give meaning to living. Belonging is important; if we belong to no one, or if those we belong to no longer care, there may be little reason to live.

STAGES LEADING TO ACCEPTANCE OF DEATH

All of us look back from time to time on our lives in an effort to assess where we are and where we have been in order to determine where we are going. The elderly, too, become involved in a process called the life review in which the past is reviewed, reassessed, reintegrated, and reconciled. If life has been put in proper perspective, the future years will be more meaningful and death easier. Some find that life was a waste of time and feelings of guilt, anxiousness, and depression develop. Those who are able to review the past, honestly evaluate and reconcile successes and failures, and develop a plan for the future are at ease with themselves and with others. The remaining years become more meaningful, life more enjoyable, and death is accepted as a part of life.

In the past decade death has become a topic of increasing investigation, discussion, and concern. An outstanding contributor in the field of thanatology (the study of death) is Elisabeth Kubler-Ross, who, after interviewing over 200 terminally ill persons and their families, described the process experienced both by the dying and by those close to them as one involving five stages (35). Although these stages have not been empirically demonstrated and are not accepted by all, they have been useful in focusing attention on dying as a process, in stimulating research, and as a helpful perspective for many practitioners.

Denial (shock) is the first stage following the announcement of approaching death. In an attempt to come to grips with the diagnosis, other medical opinions are sought, treatment may be rejected, test results are questioned, or no reference at all is made to the illness. Kubler-Ross discovered that most persons move beyond this stage before death ensues.

Anger, the second stage, is expressed when dying is perceived as a reality. The life and health of others becomes a constant reminder of one's own dying and resentment may be shown toward the living. Outbursts at family, friends, and caretakers and discontent with food and care received may all be manifestations of this anger. Concerned caring coupled with understanding without retaliation helps to reinstate the person's sense of self-worth and build feelings of acceptance of impending death.

In the third stage, *bargaining,* various attempts are made to waylay death. During this time, bargaining with God is often used in an attempt to prolong life or to gain a comfortable, non-painful death. The patient's behavior becomes admirable and anger is not usually displayed during this stage. Hope remains, however, which can serve as a tremendous support and consolation.

Depression, the fourth stage, is a reaction to grieving for the impending loss of everything meaningful in life and for life itself. As the illness progresses, the patient reviews his/her life, and death is seen as inevitable. Since depression is a normal reaction to loss, this is not a time to offer meaningless platitudes to the dying person, but to listen, understand, and give support.

Acceptance, the last stage, may come after the individual has worked through the previous stages, completed unfinished business, and goodbyes have been said. Usually the dying prefer only a few persons to be with them at this time, which may be painful and disconcerting for other family members and friends who wish to be close until the end. Death is more difficult if we, the living, hold on and do not permit the dying to die in peace. In a research study conducted by clergy of several faiths it was found that the main challenge the dying person faced was to accept or not accept the reality of death and to find value as a person in the process of dying—in its pain, loss, separation, and helplessness (36).

Hope is essential throughout the dying process, for without it living is meaningless. Hope may be for a cure, a painless death, acceptance by loved ones, support from those who are around, that death may not occur alone, that religious needs are met, and that care is given with openness, respect, honesty, and love. If hope can be maintained, dying may be supported and meaningful.

Research data indicate that most elderly persons fear prolonged illness, dependency, and pain more than death itself, but variables such as religious convictions, security in the family, immediacy of death, and institutionalization all influence the responses obtained in research studies. More substantial research is needed in this area.

Everyone wishes to die with some degree of dignity and preferably with those we love. Yet two-thirds or more of the deaths in the United States take place away from home in institutional settings where rigid visiting hours are enforced,

visitors are restricted, and conformity to institutional regula-
tions are imposed. The attitudes of many nurses, doctors, and
other health caregivers toward the terminally ill patient are not
always positive. Death is often a threat to the professional
whose goal is curing, as well as a reminder of what the future
holds for all of us. Care may then be given in a business-like
manner, with the most attention given to tubes, machines, and
procedures; in such a context the personal, psychosocial needs
of the dying person are ignored. As a consequence, many deaths
are a lonely, depersonalized, undignified experience, both for
the dying and for those left behind. Numerous experiences with
the dying and their relatives bear out the pain and helplessness
so many have to endure.

CARE OF THE DYING

Education in the care of the dying has been conspiciously
absent in medical and nursing schools until recently, when some
have begun to include this topic in the curriculum. In the past
few years, however, an intensified interest and concern for the
dying has evolved. Seminars, workshops, and courses on death
and dying are being offered and are attended by health
caregivers. It is to be hoped that continued efforts in this direction will reverse our culture's orientation toward the denial of
death so that people can die in an atmosphere of support,
understanding, and caring.

In this day of so many advances in medical technology, the
prolongation of life has become an issue of increasing concern
for the elderly. When illness strikes, complex life-supporting
measures (heroic measures) are often used that may result in undue pain, suffering, and expense. Through a Living Will, which
is distributed by the Euthanasia Educational Council (see Appendix C for address), a person can indicate to his/her physician, lawyer, and family whether or not he/she wishes heroic

measures to be taken if illness should make it impossible for the person to communicate this information in any other way.

THE HOSPICE MOVEMENT

Another relatively recent example of increasing concern for the dying is the hospice, a unique kind of care facility for the terminally ill that was revised about 30 years ago at St. Christopher's Hospice in England under Cicely Saunders' medical direction. The hospice provides a special kind of comprehensive program for the dying and their survivors that includes both palliative medical measures and emotional support. Through the efforts of a team, which usually includes a physician, nurses, social workers, clergy, and a psychiatrist as well as volunteers, the physical, psychological, spiritual, and social needs of the dying are met by a group of caring persons.

Curing of disease is not the goal of hospice care but rather the treatment of symptoms in an effort to make life meaningful and painless to the end. Pain and symptom control receive high priority. Special pain control regimens are prescribed that may include medications called Brompton's and Hospice mixture, which, when given regularly and in combination with other drugs, usually control pain and permit the dying person to be alert. Psychological and physical symptoms are treated with appropriate drugs, and comprehensive personal, psychological, and social care are provided. Treatment modalities such as intravenous feedings, resuscitation, extensive laboratory studies, intubations, and regular assessment of vital signs are usually not part of the care regimen.

The hospice model provides for both at-home and institutional care. The dying are encouraged to remain at home if someone is there to administer care as taught by the hospice staff. Around the clock, seven days a week, hospice staff are available to make house calls or to attend the dying in special in-patient settings. The hospice staff assess problems, carry out interventions, and try to meet the psychosocial needs of both patient and survivors. After death a bereavement follow-up program continues until the survivors have made a reasonable adjustment to the loss. Visits, phone calls, group sessions, letters, and regular meetings all lend support to the survivors.

Since relatives and friends are an integral part of the hospice model and not peripheral bystanders, visitors are welcome at any time. Children and pets may visit, meals are shared, and in some instances even overnight accommodations may be available. The life style of the family is respected and every effort is made to recognize needs and provide care based on individual concerns.

The hospice movement is developing and growing in the United States and offers new hope for a dignified, meaningful death. Death for the elderly should be the culmination of a life well lived. Will we provide the opportunity for this kind of death to become a reality?

BIBLIOGRAPHY

Books

Browning, Mary H. and Lewis, Edith P., eds. *The Dying Patient: A Nursing Perspective.* New York: American Journal of Nursing Company, 1972.

Butler, Robert and Lewis, Myrna. *Aging and Mental Health,* 2nd ed. St. Louis: Mosby, 1977.

Chaney, Patricia S., ed. *Dealing with Death and Dying,* 2nd ed. Horsham: Intermed Communications, 1976.

Epstein, Charlotte. *Nursing the Dying Patient.* Reston, Va.: Reston Publishing, 1975.

Feifel, Herman. *New Meanings of Death.* New York: McGraw-Hill, 1977.

Fulton, Robert, ed. *Death and Identity,* rev. ed. Bowie, Md.: Charles Press, 1976.

Jeffers, Frances C. and Verwoerdt, Adrian. How the old face death. In Busse, Ewald and Pfeiffer, Eric, eds., *Behavior and Adaptation in Late Life*. Boston: Little, Brown, 1969.

Kastenbaum, Robert J. *Death, Society, and Human Experiences*. St. Louis: Mosby, 1977.

Kastenbaum, Robert and Aisenberg, Ruth. *The Psychology of Death*. New York: Springer Publishing Company, 1972.

Kubler-Ross, Elisabeth. What it is like to be dying. In Wilcox, Sandra G. and Sutton, Marilyn, eds., *Understanding Death and Dying: An Interdisciplinary Approach*. Port Washington, N.Y.: Alfred Publishing Company, 1977.

Kubler-Ross, Elisabeth, ed. *Death: the Final Stage of Growth*. Englewood Cliffs, N.J.: Prentice-Hall, 1975.

Kubler-Ross, Elisabeth. *Questions and Answers on Death and Dying*. New York: MacMillan, 1974.

Kubler-Ross, Elisabeth. *On Death and Dying*. New York: Macmillan, 1969.

Morgan, John C. and Morgan, Richard L. *Psychology of Death and Dying*. Sunnyvale, Calif.: Westinghouse Learning Press, 1977.

Murray, Ruth and Zentner, Judith. *Nursing Assessment and Health Promotion Through the Life Span*. Englewood Cliffs, N.J.: Prentice-Hall, 1975.

Sell, Irene L. *Dying and Death: An Annotated Bibliography*. New York: Tiresias Press, 1977.

Periodicals

Armstrong, Margaret E. Dying and death—and life experiences of loss and gain: a proposed theory. *Nursing Forum 14:*95, 1975.

Craven, Joan and Wald, Florence S. Hospice care for dying patients. *American Journal of Nursing 75:*1816, 1975.

Dobihal, Edward F. Talk or terminal care? *Connecticut Medicine 33:*364, 1974.

Ingles, Thelma. St. Christopher's Hospice. *Nursing Outlook 22:*759, 1974.

Lamerton, R.C. The need for hospices. *Nursing Times 71:*155, 1975.

Melzack, R., Ofiesh, J.G. and Mount, B.M. The Brompton mixture: effects on pain in cancer patients. *CMA Journal 115:*125, 1976.

Plant, Janet. Finding a home for hospice care in the United States. *Long-term Care 51:*53, 1977.

Shusterman, L.R. Death and dying: a critical review of the literature. *Nursing Outlook 21:*465, 1973.

Unit 20

Afterword

According to Alexander Comfort, "Over the past 100 years the mean length of life has vastly increased through medical and economic advances, but the life span has not altered. What has happened is that more people reach the age of systems failure" (37).

Because greater numbers of people are living into older age than ever before, an accurate understanding of how body functions change with age is becoming increasingly important for all who work with the aged and for those who wish to know more about the best kind of preparation for their own old age.

What this book has attempted to convey can be summarized as follows.

●　Chronological age is not a reliable predictor of specific organ system efficiency or behavior. There is great individual variation in the rate of the aging process both among individuals of the same chronological age and also within a given individual, as some organ systems age more rapidly than others, depending upon past illnesses and stresses to systems, heredity, diet, exercise, and a host of other differentiating factors.

●　In spite of individual variations, there is some loss of reserve capacity in all organ systems of the body with age. Body organ systems generally continue to function quite adequately unless stressed, but stress results in reduced efficiency or inability to cope. Proper nutrition, exercise, pacing oneself, and regulating the environment to be maximally supportive are all positive ways to help offset the impact of physical aging in body systems.

● A characteristic behavior of older age is slowness—slowness in receiving information, slowness in processing and interpreting information, and slowness in reacting to information. Pacing oneself and manipulating the environment are excellent ways to compensate for the increased slowness of advancing age.

● Age-related physical changes increase the possibility of accidents and injury. Older persons and those working with older persons need to become more sensitive to and aware of situations that may contribute to accidents. Recovery time from accidental injury is usually longer for older people and often accidents are the first step in the transition from independence to dependence. Consequently, accidents have profound physical and psychological significance for older people's lives and every effort should be directed toward preventing them.

● Older persons are more susceptible to disease than the young. Physical changes associated with age leading to loss of body reserves increase the older person's vulnerability to illness. Greater emphasis on health maintenance education is needed rather than concentrating virtually all resources on illness care.

We do not intend, by our recitation here of the physical changes associated with aging, to overemphasize decline and deterioration as an inevitable part of growing old. Indeed, many persons are not drastically handicapped by age-related changes in their body systems and we believe others would be less impaired if they were given preventive health education and the knowledge and means to adapt most efficiently to their individual aging process. The decremental effects of age are a threat to self-image, to feelings of self-worth, and to independence, all of which are crucial to a satisfying and enjoyable life. Although physical changes are one of the realities of growing old, there are numerous ways to cope with them and to at least partially offset limitations imposed by age. We suggest that much more effort in practical gerontology should be devoted to ways of coping and adapting—to prevention and planning—than has been the case thus far.

Almost everyone has a different set of criteria for "successful aging," but most of the recipes seem to include the following basic suggestions.

1. Admit and accept the reality that aging imposes some limitations. Conserve energy, keep involved with life, make appropriate choices about use of time, and pace life realistically in accordance with your needs, desires, and abilities.

2. Be willing to change or modify your life style as necessary, especially your physical activities and social roles. Remain flexible, mentally and emotionally. Reduce stress whenever possible. Plan your life style to minimize disabilities and maximize remaining abilities.

3. Develop new standards for self-evaluation and new goals. Measure self-worth by inner values such as the quality of your human relationships, your spirituality, your appreciation of life, and not just by how much you can produce and achieve. Be a graceful receiver as well as a graceful giver. Older age can be a time of creativity and self-actualization if we choose to make it so.

"Growing old is really not so bad when you consider the alternative. If we live, we grow old, so we may as well do it as gracefully as possible. But we have to work at it. When the print gets smaller, the steps get higher and the sounds get softer, we have to make adjustments that may not come easily. If we learn to cooperate with the inevitable, life can be a joy to the very end" (38).

References

1. Hendricks, Jon and Hendricks, C. Davis. *Aging in Mass Society.* Cambridge, Mass.: Winthrop, 1977. p. 20.
2. Atchley, Robert. *The Social Forces in Later Life,* 2nd ed. Belmont, Calif.: Wadsworth, 1977, pp. 12-19.
3. Pieper, Hanns G. Aged Americans: a profile of a growing minority. In Barry, John R. and Wingrove, C. Ray, eds., *Let's Learn About Aging.* New York: Schenkman, 1977, pp. 7-10.
4. Neugarten, Bernice. The future of the young-old. *Gerontologist 15:* Part II 1975. pp. 4-9.
5. Randall, Ollie A. Aging in America today—new aspects in aging. *Gerontologist 17:* 1977, pp. 6-11.
6. Randall, ibid., pp. 10-11.
7. Bromley, D. B. *The Psychology of Human Ageing,* 2nd ed. Baltimore: Penguin, 1974, p. 9.
8. Erikson, Erik. *Childhood and Society,* 2nd ed. New York: Norton, 1963, pp. 247-274.
9. Brammer, Lawrence and Shostrom, Everett. *Therapeutic Psychology,* 3rd ed. Englewood Cliffs, N. J.: Prentice-Hall, 1977, pp. 87-100.
10. Neugarten, Bernice, Adult personality: toward a psychology of the life cycle. In Neugarten, Bernice, ed., *Middle Age and Aging.* Chicago: University of Chicago Press, 1968, pp. 137-147.
11. Neugarten, Bernice. The awareness of middle age. In Neugarten, Bernice, ed., *Middle Age and Aging.* ibid., pp. 93-98.
12. Hayflick, Leonard. Human cells and aging. *Scientific American 218:* 1968, pp. 32-37.

13. Selye, Hans. Stress and aging. *Journal of the American Geriatrics Society 18:* 1970, pp. 669-680.

14. American Medical Association. *The Wonderful Human Machine.* Chicago: American Medical Association, 1971, pp. 29-30.

15. Shanas, Ethel; Townsend, Peter; Wedderburn, Dorothy; Friis, Henning; Milhoj, Poul and Stehouver, Jan. *Old People in Three Industrial Societies.* New York: Atherton, 1968, pp. 26-27.

16. Harris, Raymond and Frankel, Lawrence J., eds., *Guide to Fitness After Fifty.* New York: Plenum, 1977, pp. 3-46.

17. Timiras, P. S. and Vernadakis, Antonia. Structural, biochemical and functional aging of the nervous system. In Timiras, P. S., eds., *Developmental Physiology and Aging.* New York: Macmillan, 1972, pp. 509-510.

18. Steen, Edwin B. and Montagu, Ashley. *Anatomy and Physiology,* Vol. 2. New York: Barnes and Noble, 1959, p. 135.

19. Agate, John. *The Practice of Geriatrics,* 2nd ed. Springfield, Ill.: Charles C Thomas, 1970, p. 189.

20. American Heart Association. *The Heart and Blood Vessels.* New York: American Heart Association, 1973. (pamphlet)

21. Brunner, Lillian S. and Suddarth, Doris S. *Textbook of Medical-Surgical Nursing,* 3rd ed. New York: Lippincott, 1975, pp. 137-138.

22. Masters, William H. and Johnson, Virginia. Human sexual response: the aging female and the aging male. In Neugarten, Bernice, ed., *Middle Age and Aging.* op cit., pp. 269-279.

23. Wasow, Mona and Loeb, Martin. Sexuality in nursing homes. In Burnside, Irene M., ed., *Sexuality and Aging.* Los Angeles: University of Southern California Press, 1975, p. 41.

24. Rao, Dodda B. Problems of nutrition in the aged. *Journal of the American Geriatrics Society 21:* 1973, p. 362.

25. deVries, Herbert A. Physiology of physical conditioning for the elderly. In Harris, Raymond and Frankel, Lawrence J., eds., *Guide to Fitness After Fifty.* New York: Plenum, 1977, pp. 47-52.

26. Frankel, Lawrence J. and Richard, Betty B. Gerokinesiatrics—a pharmacopoeia of exercises for the elderly. In Harris, Raymond and Frankel, Lawrence J., eds., *Guide to Fitness After Fifty.* ibid., pp. 299-306.

27. Hornbaker, Alice. *Preventive Care. Easy Exercises Against Aging.* New York: Drake Publishing Company, 1974, pp. 151-187.

28. Leaf, Alexander and Launois, John. *Youth in Old Age.* New York: McGraw-Hill, 1975, pp. 3-116.

29. Pfeiffer, Eric. Psychopathology and social pathology. In Birren, James E. and Schaie, K. Warner, eds., *Handbook of the Psychology of Aging*. New York: Van Nostrand Reinhold, 1977, p. 662.

30. Barns, Eleanor K., Sack, Ann and Shore, Herbert. Guidelines to treatment approaches. *Gerontologist 13:* 1973, pp. 513-527.

31. Oberleder, Muriel. Emotional breakdowns in elderly people. *Hospital and Community Psychiatry 20:* 1969, pp. 191-196.

32. Moss, Bertram B. Effective drug administration as viewed by a physician/administrator. In Davis, Richard H., ed., *Drugs and the Elderly*. Los Angeles: University of Southern California Press, 1975, p. 55.

33. Henry, Richard A. Physiological changes with aging regarding drugs. Unpublished paper presented at Conference on Interdisciplinary Approach to Rational Geriatric Drug Therapy, Austin, Texas, May, 1976.

34. Fulton, Robert and Fulton, Julie. A psychosocial aspect of terminal care: anticipatory grief. In Fulton, Robert and Bendiksen, Robert, eds., *Death and Identity*. Bowie, Md.: Charles Press, 1976, pp. 4-5.

35. Kubler-Ross, Elisabeth. *On Death and Dying*. New York: Macmillan, 1969, pp. 38-156.

36. Carey, Raymond G. Living until death: a program of service and research for the terminally ill. In Kubler-Ross, Elisabeth, ed., *Death: the Final Stage of Growth*. Englewood Cliffs, N. J.: Prentice-Hall, 1975, pp. 75-86.

37. Comfort, Alexander. Age prejudice in America. *Social Policy 7:* 1976, p. 3.

38. Nimeth, Albert J. *Grow Old Gracefully*. Chicago: Franciscan Herald Press, 1973, p. 3.

Appendices

APPENDIX A

Practical Hints for the Safety of the Aging

Vision

Increase illumination throughout the home.

Use spot lighting for reading or work.

Good lighting is especially important in stairways (particularly at the top and bottom of stairs), and in bathrooms and kitchens.

Encourage the use of night lights, especially in bathrooms and bedrooms.

Reduce glare from windows and shiny surfaces.

Have lamps and light switches positioned so lights can be turned on upon entering a room.

Magnifying glasses are useful for threading needles, reading medication instructions, etc.

Large dials or marked dials should be used on appliances and telephones. The "off" position should be clearly marked on appliances.

Emergency numbers should be written in large print and kept near the telephone.

Surfaces should be painted or carpeted so there is a clear and distinct boundary between stair steps, floor surfaces, thresholds, etc. Contrasting colors should be used.

Electrical cords, footstools, and other low objects should be kept out of walkways.

Furniture should not be moved to unfamiliar places.

Robes or other loose-fitting garments should not be worn in the kitchen, where they may catch fire or get caught in appliances.

Internal and external medications should be stored separately.

Medicines should not be taken at night without turning on the light and putting on proper glasses, if needed, to see well.

Objects on the dining table should be spaced so they are not easy to knock over if vision and coordination are impaired.

Older persons should be especially cautious about moving quickly when there are small pets or small children in the home.

Hearing

Since hearing loss is embarrassing to many people, the hard of hearing individual who only hears part of a conversation will often try to guess the rest. When a person's answers seem inappropriate for the question asked, be alert to possible hearing impairment. Ask the question in a different way.

Suspicious, paranoid-like behavior may accompany hearing loss, so make sure the person understands what you are doing or saying, and why.

Indications of hearing impairment include cupping hands to the ear, leaning forward, watching faces of speakers intently, and nodding in the affirmative whether appropriate or not.

Always speak slowly, lower the pitch of the voice, and enunciate clearly.

Face the individual so he/she can see your face and gestures.

Use gestures and facial expressions to enhance communication, not to distract.

Sometimes touching the person helps to get his/her attention before speaking.

Give basic information first; elaborate the details later.

If the message is very important such as, for instance, diet or medication information, write it down, go over it with the hard of hearing person, and leave the memo with him/her for future reference.

Taste and Smell

Remember that older persons may not be aware of changes in these sensory systems.

Failing to smell or taste spoiled food or failing to smell smoke or gas are dangerous. Be alert to these cues when visiting in the home.

Loss of variety in taste sensations may occur with age. Utilize textural and color differences in foods and separate foods on the plate so they can be more easily differentiated.

Touch and Balance

Touch is very important in ambulation as information is needed from receptors in the soles of the feet to provide information necessary for secure walking or climbing.

Encourage older persons to slow down, to walk more slowly, and to use a cane or walker if needed.   Some need to hold on to someone else when in a crowd or on uneven terrain.

Fasten all carpets and rugs firmly to the floor. Do not use rugs at the top of stairs or where flooring is uneven.

Mark or eliminate all uneven floor surfaces.

Install railings on all stairways, inside and out.

Use nonslip wax or carpeting on all floor surfaces.

Keep liquids, food, and other debris off floors.

Use railings on tubs and near toilets, and nonslip pads in showers or tubs.

Encourage the elderly to use railings, furniture, and walls to help maintain balance if they are unsteady.

Teach older persons to change body position gradually—especially in rising from a lying position, or rising from a seated position.

Teach older persons to be cautious in looking up or turning the head quickly, as such movements may produce dizziness.

Chairs should provide firm support and have solid arms useful in arising.

Pedestal tables may tip over if one presses down on them when getting up from a chair. Anchor such furniture or buy tables with four sturdy legs.

Arrange shelves so no climbing or extreme stretching is necessary, especially to get objects frequently used. Kitchens should be arranged to conserve energy and to reduce climbing, bending, stooping, and heavy lifting, but don't encourage too little activity around the home. Some climbing, bending, stooping, and lifting are good exercises to help maintain mobility and fitness. Over-exertion and strain are to be avoided.

APPENDIX B

Selected Resources Available to the Elderly

Self-Help Aids

Aids and Appliances for the Blind and Visually Impaired. (Catalog.) Published by the American Foundation for the Blind, 15 W. 16th St., New York, N.Y. 10011.

Ideas for Better Living. (Catalog.) Published by the American Foundation for the Blind, 15 W. 16th St., New York, N.Y. 10011.

Be OK Self-Help Aids. (Catalog.) Published by Fred Sammons, Inc., Box 32, Brookfield, Ill. 60513.

Bowar, Miriam T. (Book.) *Clothing for the Handicapped.* Minneapolis, Minn. Sister Kenny Institute, 1977.

Do It Yourself Again—Self-Help Devices for the Stroke Patient. (Booklet.) Published by the American Heart Association, 44 E. 23rd St., New York, N.Y. 10010.

Fashion Able-Self-Help Aids for Independent Living. (Catalog.) Published by Fashion Able, Rocky Hill, N.J. 08553.

May, Elizabeth, Waggoner, Neva and Hotte, Eleanor, B. *Independent Living for the Handicapped and the Elderly.* (Book.) Boston, Mass. Houghton-Mifflin, 1974.

Safety

Older Adult Pedestrian Safety. (Pamphlet.) Published by the American Automobile Association, Traffic Engineering and Safety Department, Washington, D.C. 20006.

Byerts, Thomas, ed., *Environmental Research and Aging.* (Book.) Washington, D.C.: Gerontological Society, 1974.

Diamond, Beverly, ed., *Furniture Requirements for Older People.* (Book.) New York, N.Y.: National Council on Aging, 1963.

Handle Yourself with Care. (Pamphlet.) Published by the Home Department, National Safety Council, 425 N. Michigan Ave., Chicago, Ill. 60611.

Safety of the Elderly Program Kit. A Community Program for Safer Homes, Safer Living, Safer Communities. (Program kit.) Published by the National Safety Council, 425 N. Michigan Ave., Chicago, Ill. 60611.

Safety Measures are Living Treasures. A Program Kit on Safety and Health for the Pre-retirement and Retirement Years. (Program kit.) Published by the Council on Family Health, 485 Madison Ave., New York, N.Y. 10022.

Your Retirement Safety Guide. (Pamphlet.) Published by the American Association of Retired Persons, 215 Long Beach Road, Long Beach, Calif. 90802.

APPENDIX C

Organizations from Which a Variety of Additional Information on Aging Can Be Obtained

Administration on Aging
U. S. Department of Health, Education, and Welfare
Washington, D.C. 20201

Alexander Graham Bell Association for the Deaf
1537 - 35th Street N.W.
Washington, D.C. 20201

Allergy Foundation of America
801 Second Avenue
New York, N.Y. 10017

American Academy of Dermatology
2250 N.W. Flanders Street
Portland, Or. 92710

American Association of Retired Persons
1909 K Street, N.W.
Washington, D.C. 20049

American Cancer Society
219 E. 42nd Street
New York, N.Y. 10017

American Dental Association
211 East Chicago Avenue
Chicago, Ill. 60611

American Diabetes Association,
Inc.
18 East 48th St.
New York, N.Y. 10017

American Dietetic Association
620 N. Michigan Avenue
Chicago, Ill. 60611

American Foundation for the
Blind
15 W. 16th Street
New York, N.Y. 10011

American Geriatrics Society
10 Columbus Circle
New York, N.Y. 10019

American Heart Association
44 E. 23rd St.
New York, N.Y. 10010

American Lung Association
1740 Broadway
New York, N.Y. 10019

American National Red Cross
17th and D. Street, N.W.
Washington, D.C. 20006

American Nursing Home Association
1200 15th St., N.W.
Washington, D.C. 20005

American Parkinson Disease
Foundation
147 East 50th Street
New York, N.Y. 10022

American Printing House for
the Blind, Inc.
1839 Frankfort Ave.
Louisville, Ky. 40206

American   Rehabilitation
Foundation
1800 Chicago Ave.
Minneapolis, Minn. 55404

American Speech and Hearing
Association
9030 Old Georgetown Rd.
Washington, D.C. 20014

The Arthritis Foundation
1212 Avenue of the Americas
New York, N.Y. 10036

Division for the Blind and
Physically Handicapped
Library of Congress
Washington, D.C. 20542

Epilepsy Foundation of America
Suite 406
1828 L St. N.W.
Washington, D.C. 20036

Euthanasia Educational Council
Room 831
250 West 57 Street
New York, N.Y. 10019

Gerontological Society
Suite 520
One Dupont Circle
Washington, D.C. 20036

Goodwill Industries of America, Inc.
9200 Wisconsin Avenue
Washington, D.C. 20014

Institute of Rehabilitation Medicine
400 East 34th Street
New York, N.Y. 10016

International Association of
Laryngectomees
219 E. 42nd St.
New York, N.Y. 10017

Leukemia Society of America,
Inc.
211 E. 43rd St.
New York, N.Y. 10017

Myasthenia Gravis Foundation, Inc.
New York Academy of Medicine Bldg.
2 East 103rd St.
New York, N.Y. 10029

National Association for the Deaf
814 Thayer Avenue
Silver Spring, Md. 20910

National Cancer Institute
Information Office
Bethesda, Md. 20014

National Council of Senior Citizens
1511 K. St., N.W.
Washington, D.C. 20005

National Council on the Aging
1828 L St. N.W.
Washington, D.C. 20036

National Heart and Lung Institute
National Institutes of Health
Bethesda, Md. 20014

National Institute of Arthritis, Metabolism and Digestive Diseases
National Institutes of Health
Bethesda, Md. 20014

National Institute of Neurological Disease and Stroke
National Institutes of Health
Bethesda, Md. 20014

National Kidney Foundation
116 East 27thSt.
New York, N.Y. 10016

National Multiple Sclerosis Society
257 Park Ave. South
New York, N.Y. 10010

National Paraplegia Foundation
333 North Michigan Avenue
Chicago, Ill. 60601

National Parkinson Foundation, Inc.
1501 N.W. 9th Avenue
Miami, Fl. 33136

National Rehabilitation Association
Suite 1120
1550 K. St., N.W.
Washington, D.C. 20005

National Society for the Prevention of Blindness
16 East 58th Street
New York, N.Y. 10016

Parkinson's Disease Foundation
640 West 168th St.
New York, N.Y. 10032

Recording for the Blind, Inc.
121 E. 58th St.
New York, N.Y. 10022

Rehabilitation International
219 E. 44th St.
New York, N.Y. 10017

Rehabilitation Services Administration
Department of Health, Education, and Welfare
330 C St., S.W.
Washington, D.C. 20201

United Ostomy Association
1111 Wilshire Blvd.
Los Angeles, Calif. 90017

Index

DATE DUE

OCT 6 1986		
APR 1 3 1987		
DEC 1 9 1988		
ILL 6/2/89		